THE
Jesus Prayer

A CRY FOR MERCY,
A PATH OF RENEWAL

JOHN MICHAEL TALBOT

IVP Books

An imprint of InterVarsity Press
Downers Grove, Illinois

InterVarsity Press
P.O. Box 1400, Downers Grove, IL 60515-1426
World Wide Web: www.ivpress.com
Email: email@ivpress.com

InterVarsity Press® is the book-publishing division of InterVarsity Christian Fellowship/USA®, a movement of students and faculty active on campus at hundreds of universities, colleges and schools of nursing in the United States of America, and a member movement of the International Fellowship of Evangelical Students. For information about local and regional activities, write Public Relations Dept., InterVarsity Christian Fellowship/USA, 6400 Schroeder Rd., P.O. Box 7895, Madison, WI 53707-7895, or visit the IVCF website at www.intervarsity.org.

All Scripture quotations, unless otherwise indicated, are taken from the The Holy Bible, New King James Version. Copyright © 1982 by Thomas Nelson, Inc.

Scripture quotations marked RNAB are taken from the New American Bible with Revised New Testament and Revised Psalms © 1991, 1986, 1970 Confraternity of Christian Doctrine, Washington, D.C., and are used by permission of the copyright owner. All rights reserved. No part of the New American Bible may be reproduced in any form without permission in writing from the copyright owner.

While all stories in this book are true, some names and identifying information in this book have been changed to protect the privacy of the individuals involved.

Cover design: Cindy Kiple
Interior design: Beth Hagenberg

Images: cross: © zoran simin/iStockphoto
*   rough white wall: © mrfotos/iStockphoto*

ISBN 978-0-8308-3577-5 (print)
ISBN 978-0-8308-9558-8 (digital)

Printed in Canada ∞

Library of Congress Cataloging-in-Publication Data

Talbot, John Michael.
  The Jesus prayer : a cry for mercy, a path of renewal / John Michael Talbot.
      pages cm
  Includes bibliographical references
  ISBN 978-0-8308-3577-5 (hardcover : alk. paper)
  1. Jesus prayer. I. Title.
  BT590.J28T35 2013
  242'.72—dc23

                                                      2013014791

P	19	18	17	16	15	14	13	12	11	10	9	8	7	6	5	4	3	2	1
Y	29	28	27	26	25	24	23	22	21	20	19	18	17	16	15	14	13			

"Lord, Jesus Christ, Son of God,

have mercy on me, a sinner."

❖

Contents

Introduction

I discovered the Jesus Prayer at a time in my life when I desperately needed something to deepen my life in Christ.

After reading about the various major world religions, I rediscovered Jesus Christ while reading the Revised Standard Bible that my dear Methodist grandmother had given me for the confirmation I did not receive. I had wandered away from Christianity into rock 'n' roll, but had come back after seeing firsthand that most of the stars who had everything I thought I wanted were really still very empty and unhappy. This led me to Jesus at the height of the Jesus Movement. Eventually I ended up recording Jesus music with Sparrow Records, a company that has since become the largest Christian recording company in the world.

But I was empty. I had memorized much of the Bible and

had become a proverbial "Bible thumper," but I had lost some of the simple Jesus I briefly experienced in the first days of my return to Christ. My Christian life began to bottom out. Then I discovered the early church fathers, or patristics, and began to study them. This led me to the monastic and Franciscan doorway to the Orthodox tradition and on to the Catholic faith. But this did not cut me off from my evangelical past. Rather, it enlivened it! Ironically, my Methodist grandmother once told me, "Johnny, now that you are Catholic I think you are a better Methodist than *ever!*"

I encountered the Jesus Prayer early on in a book called *The Way of the Pilgrim.* I was also reading Thomas Merton's books and others like *The Imitation of Christ* and *The Cloud of Unknowing.* I was reading monastic sources like "The Sayings of the Desert Fathers" and various Franciscan books. I was then led to the Philokalia, or "the study of the beautiful," which is a collection of sources from the Christian East.

The Jesus Prayer is a big part of Eastern spirituality. I must admit that I related more to the Western tradition, which came from a culture that more recently and directly gave birth to mine. It used a language that seemed more approachable. And I found that the Franciscan tradition went back to the gospel with a gentle but fierce directness that I liked.

Not long after I became the founder of a new integrated monastic community, the Brothers and Sisters of Charity, a child of our Franciscan mother in the Catholic Church. I immersed myself in the Christian East and the West. After a period of some dryness and disappointment I entered into an extended period of more intense solitude in my monastic cell, and began to restudy interfaith sources on monasticism and meditation. I also reinstituted an intensive daily practice of meditation. After ten or so years, and really allowing that stream to find its place in my Catholic Christian faith, I began to use and teach the Jesus Prayer with a whole new confidence.

Specifically, I encountered a deepening of my faith from the understandable things of faith and morality to a more habitual experience of God in contemplative grace beyond understanding, names, forms and description. Using traditional disciplines of asceticism and meditation, I found myself breaking through to contemplation with my spirit, which is part of the Catholic Christian heritage.

THE GIFT OF THE MYSTICAL TRADITION

In the monastic and Franciscan Catholic and Orthodox streams I discovered the contemplative and mystical traditions of which the Jesus Prayer is a vital expression. This enlivened my faith in a way I had hungered for but had not found very often in my experience. After that, new richness and vast horizons began to open up.

Many evangelical Protestants, and those of all expressions, have experienced something similar. We learn the Scriptures almost by heart. We learn much with our heads, but somehow the heart remains empty. Our salvation experience remains only an idea or an emotional high at best. Catholics and Orthodox can do the same through the study of patristics, liturgy, sacraments, ecclesiology or canon law.

I have found that my head-oriented and dry Christian faith is not limited to me. I often hear of a hunger for something more within my own tradition. Pastors, ministers and students find that once they are in active ministry, they begin to burn out because mere intellectual training and emotional experiences are not enough to sustain them. The very best expression of that "something more"—the Jesus Prayer—is from the monastic Christian East. But it has something for us all, East or West, secular or monastic.

Different traditions have tried to explain the mystical experience using various paradigms. After rather extensive experience of the meditation described in the Christian West, East and Far Eastern religions from a Christian perspective, I found the Pauline paradigm of spirit, soul and body worked best for me as a follower of Jesus. The body is the senses, emotions and thoughts of the brain. The soul is the spiritual mind or reason. The spirit is the place of passive contemplation.

The problem is that through sin we often get stuck in a self-identity that is limited to our senses, emotions and thoughts. The spirit remains asleep. We are forgiven and empowered to holiness in Christ through the cross and resurrection. When the old self dies with Christ, then the spirit is reborn in his Spirit through the cross and resurrection of Christ, and we become an entirely new person. This is a breakthrough, liberation and rebirth in the fullest sense in Jesus!

But it does not stop there. This breakthrough in the Spirit then permeates our entire being, enlivening the reason of the soul and the senses, emotions and thoughts of the body so they fulfill their original purpose. Now the thoughts facilitate the spirit with good doctrine, emotions empower us with enthusiasm and the body becomes the vehicle where the wonder of this new life in Christ unfolds. We are truly "born again."

A REPETITIVE PRAYER

The Jesus Prayer is a rosary. A rosary is any repetitive prayer prayed on a knotted rope or beaded cord. Anyone traveling in the Middle East has seen Orthodox monks walking through the busy markets and praying a rosary. That rosary is the Jesus Prayer.

Some might rightly point out that Jesus condemned vain repetitions. Indeed, Jesus taught us the "Lord's Prayer" or the "Our Father" specifically to teach us not to engage in vain repetitions. (Unfortunately, this sometimes happens with that very prayer when we pray too speedily.) The trick is to pray repetitions with real meaning, not to stop repetitive prayer altogether!

Many of the prayers of Orthodox Jews would have required that Jesus pray repetitive prayers. The great *Shema Yisrael* ("Hear, [O] Israel") are the first two words of a section of the Torah and comprise the title (sometimes shortened to Shema) of a prayer that serves as a centerpiece of the morning and evening Jewish prayer services. The first verse encapsulates the monotheistic essence of Judaism: "Hear, O Israel: the LORD our God, the LORD *is* one," found in Deuteronomy 6:4. *Shema* means to "hear," but in a way that is also obedient to what we hear. In English the word *obedience* comes from the Latin *oboedire*, which comes from *ob* (toward) and *oeirdire* (to hear, listen and do). Jesus certainly did not take issue with this prayer, but only in repeating it as rote ritual without right meaning and right intention, and as a genuine prayer.

So repetitive prayer is not the problem. Vain repetition is.

BREATH

The Eastern monastic fathers teach us to unite the Jesus Prayer to our breathing. This is often frightening to those who are skeptical of uniting prayer with the breath due to its similarity with Eastern meditation. But there is a good reason for this teaching, which is similar to but distinct from the teaching of Eastern religions.

The words for Spirit in Scripture are *rûaḥ* in Hebrew and *pneuma* in Greek. Both mean "air, wind and breath," specifically the air, wind and breath of a rational creature. In order to get a full breath of air we must relearn how to breathe with both lungs!

The apostle Paul instructs us to "pray without ceasing" (1 Thess 5:17). Through the centuries we have tried different ways to fulfill this. We have prayed at various times of the day through the monastic Work of God or Liturgy of the Hours, which help us to pray always.

Some, like the fourth-century Messalian Euchites, went to the absurd extreme of constant prayer to the neglect of everything else. Others, like the monks of Cluny in tenth-century Europe, established a constant rotation of monks who prayed in their churches. The notion was that, as the body of Christ, if one was praying, all were praying. Today some similarly practice "perpetual adoration" of Jesus under the exposed bread and wine on the altar. Prayer vigils are also practiced in modern Protestant traditions.

Some of the church fathers taught that after fixed times of prayer we can continue to pray inwardly throughout our daily activities as a form of continual prayer. In his *Commentary on the Psalms* St. Augustine said, "There is another inward kind of prayer without ceasing, which is the desire of the heart. Whatever activity you happen to be engaged in . . . if you only long for that Sabbath then you do not cease to pray. If you do not want to pause in prayer then never pause in your longing."

The Eastern monastic fathers taught that we can unite the Jesus Prayer with every breath. We need not be in a church or chapel, or even in a prayer space to practice this prayer. Think about it: What is the one thing we do without ceasing? We breathe. If we are not breathing, chances are we are already dead!

St. Hesychios the Priest (eighth or ninth century) said in *On Watchfulness and Holiness*: "Just as it is impossible to . . . live without breathing . . . we should use the name of Jesus as we do our own breath. Let the Jesus Prayer cleave to your breath, and in a few days you will find that it is possible [to pray without ceasing]. With your breathing combine watchfulness and the name of Jesus." So, from the perspective of praying in the breath or Spirit of God with our spirit, or of praying "without ceasing," uniting prayer with our breath works very well.

USING THIS BOOK

I have been teaching the Jesus Prayer for about a decade in retreats at our Little Portion Retreat Center, and more recently in hundreds of three-day parish missions all across America. People are responding! Most say that the Jesus Prayer helps them find a place of legitimate meditation with the use of their breath. Months and years after a particular mission I still receive encouraging communications that confirm that this Prayer has a profound effect on personal prayer life and the entire life of the church and the world. This book comes out of this experience.

Roman Catholics and Protestants appreciate the practices from the Christian East that balance our largely Western approach to faith. As we rediscover our own heritage and put it into practice, seekers will not have to look elsewhere (such as to Eastern religions) for the legitimate human need for meditative and contemplative prayer that brings health on the spiritual, psychological, emotional and physical levels of life.

The chapters of this book are formed around each word of

the prayer. Reflecting on the words will bring us into a full understanding of the words of the Jesus Prayer. After that we will pray the words with a greater intuitive grasp.

At the end of each chapter you will be invited to pray the Jesus Prayer. I encourage you to set aside a few minutes each day to begin to pray in this way.

If you want more detailed background on the origins of the Jesus Prayer, you will find an appendix at the back with further information.

It is my prayer that this book will encourage you to take a similar spiritual journey in Christ without encountering the many pitfalls and obstacles I encountered. I was helped enormously by my spiritual father. I now seek to repay that debt of love to you!

PRACTICE

The actual words of the Jesus Prayer are simple. The traditional prayer is, "Lord, Jesus Christ, Son of God, have mercy on me, a sinner." These words come mainly from Scripture and are rich in meaning, but for now let's just get used to praying them.

The Jesus Prayer is united with the breath in two motions: the in breath and the out breath. Breathing in we say, "Lord, Jesus Christ, Son of God." Breathing out we say, "Have mercy on me, a sinner."

Originally, the Prayer concluded with "Son of God." The words "have mercy on me, a sinner" were added later for the novices (new monks). The young of ancient tradition were not that different from young converts today who sometimes think they have the answers that their elders have missed. The Eastern monastic elders added these words to keep the young novices in their place!

Breathing this Prayer for a few minutes we will begin to notice an almost natural motion. Breathing in fills us up, and breathing out empties us. Breathing in causes us to hold on, and breathing out causes us to let go.

This works well with the actual meaning of the words. The first words fill us with all that is beautiful: the personal lordship of Jesus, personal salvation, the anointing of the Spirit, the Trinity, the incarnation, the church and the sacraments. The second group of words causes us to let go of anything standing between us and full communion with God through Jesus and with all people.

This letting go is most powerful. We are often filled with all kinds of rationalizations and justifications about why we are not in full communion with God and the church. While these might make sense or may be largely correct, they will never free us from our ego attachments to our opinions and agendas regarding God, the church, others and ourselves. Breathing out is a powerful tool for letting go.

Take a few minutes and practice this. Sit straight but comfortably. Breathe deeply through your nose, but not artificially. Allow yourself to fill up with God, and then let go of anything standing between you and full communion with God through Christ (or the church as a body or as individuals).

The Way of the Pilgrim says, "Now if you will listen, I will read how you can learn ceaseless interior prayer." The elder opened the Philokalia to the account of St. Simeon the New Theologian and began reading:

> Sit alone and in silence; bow your head and close your eyes; relax your breathing and with your imagination look into your heart; direct your thoughts from your head into your heart. And while inhaling say, "Lord Jesus Christ, have mercy on me," either softly with your lips or in your mind. Endeavor to fight distractions but be patient and peaceful and repeat this process frequently.

St. Calistas and Ignatius in their work *Directions to Hesychasts* also say:

> Sitting down in your cell, collect your mind, lead into the path of your breath along which the air enters in, constrain it to enter the heart together with the air, and keep it there. Keep it there, and do not leave it silent or idle; instead give it the following prayer: "Lord, Jesus Christ, Son of God, have mercy on me." Let this be its constant occupation.

1

Lord

*T*he words of the Jesus Prayer are important. But they are not the most important. The fathers call this "Prayer of the Heart." When we pray the Prayer we use the faculty of intuition to grasp its realities. But we cannot intuit them if we do not have at least a basic understanding of what the words actually mean. Let's walk through the words briefly so that we can immerse ourselves in the deeper meanings of the Prayer later.

LORD

The first word in The Jesus Prayer is *Lord*. There are several Hebrew and Greek words in Scripture that are used of God. Of course, they all go back to YHWH, or the Tetragrammaton, a Greek word meaning "the four letters," the actual name of God which was not to be pronounced by the human tongue, according to the Jews. God remains transcendent, beyond all human thought and words. Thus, in place of the Tetragrammaton, Adonai, Jehovah or Lord have been inserted.

The incomprehensibility of God is brought out in the apophatic Christian tradition, which is also spoken of by the Greek philosophers. They say that what we can say about God is next to nothing compared to what we cannot know with the mind or describe with human words. This is the realm of paradoxes or apparent contradictions that speak deeper truths. Here silence sometimes speaks best of the eternal Word.

The Greek word is more understandable. It is *kyrios*, which means "supreme in authority, controller, God, Lord and master." It is still heard today in Catholic liturgies of the East and West in the Kyrie Eleison or the "Lord Have Mercy" that begins every Mass.

While these scriptural words are indeed most interesting, I would like to focus on the derivation of the English word for Lord. The word is *hlafweard*, a thirteenth-century word which means "the maker or keeper of the bread." *Hlaf* means "loaf," and *weard* means "lord" or "master of a household, ruler, superior," also "God."

The English word *lord* goes back to the feudal system, which was set in place after the fall of the Roman Empire. Feudalism was good in that it kept Europe from lapsing into barbarianism. In that system a person called a "lord" was placed in charge of a region. The poor grew the wheat, which they brought to the local lord, who processed it into flour and bread, and distributed it to the people of his region. It was not an equal distribution, but according to need. Some needed more and some less. This was similar to the process of Acts 2 and 4. As long as the lord was good, or benevolent, it worked well. When it failed, it went terribly wrong.

Only after the lords became habitually bad did the need for a reform surface. For example, around the time of Francis of Assisi in the late twelfth and early thirteenth centuries, the town of Assisi adopted the new democratic capitalism. In this new system the poor could rise from poverty through hard work and enterprise, and become successful in business. Successful merchants were often elected to positions of leadership in the community. Francis's father, Pietro Bernardone, was one of these successful merchants. However, despite his rise to financial and social success, Pietro remained unhappy, so Francis rejected the sociopolitical answer in favor of a more spiritual one.

So, various systems work well when there are good people in leadership. The analogy of the feudal lord remains very interesting for us as we look to the real meaning of the word *Lord* in the Jesus Prayer.

THE MAKER OF THE BREAD

The process of making bread is a wonderful analogy for the Christian life. Life is filled with challenges, but also rewards! While there are sacrifices along the way, if we stay with it we end up being transformed into a wonderful loaf of bread that can nourish others and ourselves.

Unprocessed wheat is good, but it must be processed into flour and dough, and baked into bread before it can be eaten and digested in a way that will nourish a human body. Unprocessed grains of wheat are nice as filler in modern wheat bread, but we cannot eat raw wheat alone. It will actually make us sick, and we will subsequently throw up. Wheat must be processed before it is nourishing.

HARVESTED WHEAT

Wheat begins as a stalk growing in a wheat field. Anyone who has seen a wheat field knows its beauty. The wheat stalks blow gracefully in the winds of the Great Plains, shining golden in the sun. Like the wheat stalk, it would be easy for us to think, *I am beautiful just as I am. Leave me be!* But we must be cut down and harvested like wheat to be transformed into nourishing bread.

It is true that a good God creates us all in the very image of God. All human beings are created to seek goodness, truth, beauty, justice, love and all things good. We are all given natural gifts that are good. These things are beautiful in and of themselves. The problem is that we do not always use them for good. St. Thomas Aquinas says that we must do "the right thing rightly." Unfortunately, we do not. This is called sin, *hamartia*, "missing the mark," in Greek. Because of our sin, we lose the likeness of God. But the fathers of the church say that we never lose that residual image that still hungers for God.

So, the natural stalk of wheat must be cut down in order to transform the wheat into nourishing bread. It must be cut at the base, and cut all the way through. Otherwise, the stalk will tear and the grain will not be clean enough for use. In the same way we can hold on to nothing of the old self. Even hanging on to one bit of the old self keeps us from being usable for the process of making bread.

The process that transforms us is the cross of Christ. Jesus asks us to let go of three things: possessions, relationships and our very self (Lk 14:25-33). This is not because the created world or possessions, relationships with friends and family, and our self is bad. But we have used good things badly! Often our possessions posses us. We enable negative relationships through codependency or control, and our self-identity is incomplete or false. We walk with these wrong uses of right things throughout our lives, and the habits become deeply ingrained and are most difficult to change.

The only way to break free of these old ingrained patterns is to renounce these things completely. That renunciation occurs through the cross of Christ. When we renounce these old patterns of self, we are born again as a completely new creation in Christ. Now we are set free! We can use created possessions instead of them enslaving us. Our relationships enhance mutual empowerment instead of negative en-ablement. And we find our self-identity in Christ, which is truly life-giving through the self-emptying of love that completely frees us from ego attachments.

THRESHING

But the process is not over, far from it. It has only just begun! Many think that completely letting go of the old self through the cross of Christ is something they might achieve toward the end of their Christian lives. While there is truth to that because we never stop growing in Christ throughout our lives, we often rob ourselves of the new life Jesus wants for us by postponing renunciation of the old self. However, Jesus teaches us that such renunciation is only the beginning. This is seen in the further process of making a loaf of bread, of letting Jesus really be the Lord of our lives.

What happens after we cut down a stalk of wheat? It must be threshed, which removes the grain and shell of wheat from the stalk. By beating the cut stalks on a tarp, we collect the shell and grain within. This is violent, but not so violent as to do harm to the shell and grain of wheat.

Do you ever feel a bit threshed in your daily life? I know I do! Sometimes we feel that the daily challenges of life continually thresh us. But it must be done in order to remove the shell and grain from the old stalk of our life. Only then can we be turned into God's bread.

The Little Portion Monastery in Arkansas had a terrible fire in 2008. Immediately after the fire the Great Recession hit our nation and the entire world. It was a terrible time to try to raise money to rebuild. But we did. Recently our community opened St. Clare's Monastery in Houston. In the current recession it made more sense to purchase an existing property, so we found a lovely place on two acres in the city—a great deal. But we have discovered that the house needed many repairs! After one thing is fixed, we discover another! We now have twenty-six pages of repairs. But we have been most fortunate to have a great community of local supporters from Prince of Peace parish and the greater Houston area who have come to our rescue to get this monastic house up and running. While not a proverbial "money pit," it has made us feel like we have been threshed! Everyone has their own version of this.

WINNOWING

After being threshed, we must be winnowed. When winnowing, we throw the shell and grain into the air and let the wind separate the "wheat and the chaff" (Mt 3:12). In our lives, the wind is the Spirit (Jn 3:8). The wind blows the lighter chaff, or shell, from the heavier grain of wheat. The chaff blows away, and the grain of wheat falls back into the tarp. Today this is done by machinery, but the principle remains the same. The wind must separate the wheat and the chaff before the wheat can be used to make bread.

Do you ever feel a bit "up in the air"? I know I do! This often happens at retirement or when our last child moves out of the house. Divorce, a terrible time of having everything considered stable being taken from us, is another example. Recently, financial decline has left many of us feeling so far up in the air that we weren't sure when or where we would land.

The music business dropped 70 percent in the years immediately following the onset of the recession. That is bankruptcy in anyone's business plan! Top 20 artists were okay, dropping from hundreds of millions to tens of millions in sales. Middle artists like myself were hit very hard. Add to that the transition from CDs to digital sales, where 95 percent were still being downloaded illegally, and the normal older-artist syndrome, where sales slowly drop off, and the music ministry I had known for thirty years was completely changed in a matter of months. I was totally "up in the air"!

But I was being winnowed. I had a choice: stay in the old model and die, or find a new way of ministry in Christ. I chose the latter, and am doing better than I have ever done before. We now use itinerant ministry in parish missions throughout the United States. Instead of large ticketed events, our team now goes to parishes big and small, and brings the gospel for a simple free-will offering. I feel free as a bird and would never go back to the old model. I realize that I once felt trapped in the cage of "the relig biz." Now I am free to do more authentic ministry that is radically changing lives for the better in Christ.

So don't be afraid of being winnowed and feeling a bit up in the air. It is an opportunity to be fanned by the wind of the Spirit of God and released from the shell of the old self. When we let go and let God, then the grain of wheat will be exposed and fall back to the ground where it can be used for the nourishment of all.

GROUND INTO FLOUR

After all this you'd think we would be finished, but we're not! There is still more work to do. In order for the grain to be usable for baking bread, it must be crushed and ground into flour. For this, a grinding stone is used.

In Capernaum, or Kfar Nahum, the "village of Nahum" (not the biblical prophet), on the north shore of the Sea of Galilee in the Holy Land there is such a grinding stone. They are immense, almost a yardstick wide and as big around as a man is tall. A grain of wheat caught under this stone is completely crushed. Likewise it would be deadly to a human being.

This is exactly the point! The old self must die with Christ so that the new self can be born again in the resurrection of Jesus. Notice that none of the basic "stuff" of the wheat is lost. It is simply reconstituted. It is re-formed.

I went through this with my music ministry back in 1978. I left the rock 'n' roll world of country rock music with a secular band named Mason Proffit. We had enjoyed moderate success and were considered pioneers of that genre. We were one of those "almost famous" bands that litter the music world. But I left the band a few years after I came back to Jesus in 1971 with the Jesus Movement. At first I was part of the tail end of the first generation of Jesus music. I used my country rock talents to make music for Christ, and did fairly well. But I was not reaching folks the way I felt called to do.

One night in Denver I ministered with my friend Barry McGuire. He had a great stage presence, but never really played or sang all that well from a technical perspective. But the Holy Spirit worked though him like I had never seen before. So I asked him what he did. He said something that changed my life: "Make music for God, and let God take care of the people because he can do it better than you can."

Now I make music completely unlike anything I was trained for. I was trained for country rock. Now I make sacred and meditational folk classical music. It has reached millions, where before it reached tens of thousands. It took off, where before I was trying to get it off the ground. It went from crawling to flying in the Spirit! But none of my basic talents were wasted. All of them were used. But it had to be completely reformed into something I would never have dreamed of or imagined. Then it could be used by God for greater things.

We all have our version of how this has or could happen in our lives. When we let go of all that we are, then Jesus can turn us into someone completely new and use all that we are for God. We will also find ourselves completely fulfilled in the process. We will go from wheat to nourishing and life-giving bread.

DOUGH

In the process of turning our flour into dough, we need encouragement in the midst of facing the crosses that transform us along with the resurrection.

First the Lord adds the water of the Spirit to empower us for doing his work, and the salt of the Word to preserve us in hard times. He also adds yeast so that we might rise after our crucifixions. These things bring us encouragement in the midst of the process. Like Jesus, who experienced the transfiguration (Mt 17) to encourage him and the apostles before the crucifixion, even as we pass through dry times and crosses in our lives on earth we are encouraged by God's graces that give us a foretaste of the eventual resurrection. The Christian life is not all testing, trials and crosses!

But the dough must be flattened, rolled and worked to be ready for the baking process. Do you ever feel flattened, rolled and overworked in life? Do not despair. Relax and roll with it! It is all part of our rebirth in Christ.

RISING IN THE PAN

Next we are put into a pan and allowed to rise. Again there are negative and positive elements in this part of the process.

Being placed in a pan can seem restrictive. We may not like being reshaped. We grow comfortable with the shape we are in! But Jesus wants us to be conformed to his image and likeness through both the suffering of the cross and the glory of his resurrection (Phil 3:10, 21). He does not want us to be conformed to the patterns of this passing world, but to him through a whole new way of thinking (Rom 12:20)! This can put a real cramp in our former way of thinking and acting. It is a radical change. But it must be done. This is all part of being reformed.

Then we are set aside a bit to rise up through the action of the leaven in the dough of our life. This can seem a time of inactivity. But relax and let yourself slowly rise. A whole new form in Christ is emerging. At times like these we need the faith to be patient with the process.

As we are rising we are poked and we fall flat again! But it's okay. We are rising up again. We say, "I am a person of the resurrection, so I am rising up again!" What then? We get poked again! This happens three times in the rising process. What if this isn't allowed to happen? We get put into the oven and we blow up! Poking the dough in the midst of the rising process may seem discouraging, but it is for our own good. Without it we will never become a golden-brown loaf of bread.

THE OVEN

We approach the end of the bread-making process by being placed in the oven. This is a trial by fire spoken of in 1 Peter 4:12, and it is hot as blazes in there! Fire is used throughout Scripture as a symbol of both trial and love. It is a symbol of the Holy Spirit (Mt 3:12; Acts 2:3). Fire tests the quality of each one's works (1 Cor 3:13). It is also used for destruction in the final judgment of God and of hell (Mt 7:19; 13:40) St. Bonaventure often calls it the fire of God. St. John of the Cross said that the fire is a given, but it is our approach to the fire of God that makes all the difference. We can either resist the fire and find it uncomfortable, or embrace it and find it comforting.

The same thing is true with making bread. We can either resist and lose our peace, or relax and let ourselves be baked in the oven. Then, we will be transformed into a golden-brown, warm loaf of bread.

COOLING

The last step in this process is cooling down. A loaf of bread fresh out of the oven cannot be eaten immediately. It must cool down a bit. It must just sit and be still. There has been a lot of activity. Now it is time to rest. But this resting makes the loaf edible, though it is best when still warm.

The same is true for us. After all the activity of making the new loaf of our lives, we must rest and cool down a bit before we can really serve others. This is the contemplative stage of our lives. We do a lot of dying and rising to be fully converted. But we must also learn to be still before we can really be nourishing for others. We must learn the contemplative graces before we are ready for effective ministry. We must allow ourselves to be transformed into a presentable loaf of bread before we can be nourishing for others.

CONCLUSION

These are just a few reflections on Jesus being the Lord of our lives. As we pray the Jesus Prayer, this entire process is in-

tuited on a level much deeper than mere discursive meditation. It drops from the head to the heart. It builds on the
thoughts and emotions of meditation and becomes an intuited contemplation that surpasses them all. That is one of
the gifts of the Jesus Prayer.

PRACTICE

As we breathe in the word *Lord*, we allow Jesus to really be
the Lord of our lives. We allow ourselves to fill up completely
with the reality of being completely remade and remolded in
the likeness of Jesus. Bring the old self, the unprocessed
wheat of our gifts and talents, to the cross and let it go. Then
allow a completely new person to rise up in the resurrection
of Jesus. We allow ourselves to become a healthy and nourishing loaf of bread in Jesus, the Bread of Life.

<u>2</u>

Jesus

Lord, *Jesus* . . .

*T*he next word in the Jesus Prayer is the name above all other names: Jesus. His name means "savior" and was given to several people in Scripture.

The word in Hebrew is *Yĕhôšûa*, Jehoshua. It means "Jehovah is salvation." It was the name of Joshua, successor to Moses as the leader of the children of Israel. In Greek it is *Iēsous* and was the proper name of Jesus Christ, the Savior of the world.

There is a spirituality to names. Names are both the reality of a person and only the external symbol of a deeper person beyond mere names. We know that in heaven our earthly names will be replaced by a name that is now secret and will only be known to each of us (Rev 2:17). The same is true for Jesus. *Jesus* is a symbol of the deep personal reality of the incarnate Logos, but it is only a symbol. At the same time it is, like the sacrament of the Eucharist, both the symbol and the Real Presence of the reality it symbolizes. When we pray the Jesus Prayer, this mystery unfolds in a way that is both knowable and beyond complete human understanding.

SALVATION AND SAVIOR

We speak and hear the words *salvation* and *savior* all the time, especially in Christianity. It is all through the Scriptures we read and the sermons and homilies we hear. Churches that follow lectionary readings hear the word proclaimed in the continual rotation of Scripture that takes us through the entire Bible annually in daily reading and every three years on Sundays. We also hear Scripture in the various liturgies of the church, especially in the Catholic Mass or in what many Protestants call the order of worship.

But this almost constant use of these words can numb us to their power. Salvation assumes that we know that we are lost! Often we mentally assent to this, but fail to grasp it on the level of the heart. We grow religious calluses around our hearts that make genuine heartfelt perception of salvation nearly impossible. It also makes genuine compassion for others difficult as well.

People in twelve-step programs have an incredible grasp of

the gospel. The very first step is to admit that we are totally powerless and need a Higher Power to save us. Otherwise we are helplessly lost. No one knows better about being lost than someone who has suffered an addiction to a deadly substance.

I am reminded of my late sister who spent most of her life in tragic drug addiction, and the lifestyle that went with it. She ended up addicted to crack cocaine. My beautiful sister, who had stunning looks and a great spirit and soul in her youth, looked old and haggard and had a manipulative personality. She once told me that there was little that she had not done in order to obtain her drugs. But a year before she died she came back to Christ and the Catholic Church. She sang in the choir and loved the folks at her parish. But her body had given out. She died in peace with her Lord, her church and her family and friends. I believe that God took her as soon as she was ready to go. Her tragic life is over and she is now enjoying the presence of God in Jesus. As I write I am close to tears at the thought of her salvation. Jesus was and is truly her Savior.

St. Bonaventure (1221–1274), sometimes called the second founder or at least the rescuer of the fledgling Franciscan Order of Friars Minor, said that we are like people who have fallen into a deep pit. Try as we may, we simply cannot climb out with our own power. We might get close to the top, but just as we think we can get out, we lose our grasp and fall back to the bottom. Bonaventure says that only Jesus can reach down with his strong and loving hands and lift us out.

Only Jesus can really save us. On our own we are unable to climb out of the pit of our sin.

I remember a friend from my band days who went on to operate a river rafting business. Once, a rafting group he was leading got hit by a flash flood. Because of the flood, rattle-snakes escaped from their dens around the river and slithered up the bank, making it nearly impossible for a group to get out of the river safely. The water rose so quickly that the group ended up clinging to some trees on a small island in the middle of the violently rising and widening river. My buddy went to shore, made it through the snakes and went for help. After what seemed to be hours he returned in a he-licopter to get the stranded rafters out of the river. By then they were clinging desperately to the very top of the tree, expecting to be washed away at any moment. But in the nick of time they were rescued, saved. Their gratitude and relief knew no bounds. They were weeping tears of joy at being snatched from the very jaws of death. These folks knew what it is to be saved. For them, my buddy and the helicopter rescue crew were saviors.

We often go through similar experiences on the spiritual level. But we often lose touch with them as time slips further away from the immediacy of the experience. Praying the Jesus Prayer and using Jesus' name keeps that salvation moment ever before our eyes.

There is a brother on Mt. Athos, in Greece, who walks up to folks and asks, "What do you think, brother, are we being saved today?" As he does so he gently weeps tears of gratitude and joy. When we properly understand our salvation and our Savior, we cannot help but weep as well. This is not something from the past or in the future. It is now! It is immediate and intimately personal.

BLOOD SACRIFICE

Christians repeatedly say that Jesus "shed his blood for the forgiveness of sins." We find this fact all through the New Testament and the eucharistic liturgy. Contemporary people, particularly those in the West, have a problem relating to the blood sacrifice. We easily understand enlightenment and liberation, but the notion of shedding blood for the remission of sins is not part of our daily life or cultural awareness. Modern Westerners may accept the need for forgiveness as a self-help reality, but fail to grasp the deeper personal and self-sacrificing aspect that comes from the Christian heritage. In this regard we are more comfortable with a Far Eastern understanding of forgiveness than the Christian teaching. The Buddhist Dhammapada says that all we have to do to be forgiven of our sins is experience liberating awakening. While this concept is something that most modern Westerners relate to, it is not nearly as costly and personal.

The best way for us to understand blood sacrifice, which was so predominant in ancient religion in general, is that blood means life. Leviticus 17:11 says, "For the life of the flesh *is* in the blood, and I have given it to you upon the altar to make atonement for your souls; for it *is* the blood *that* makes atonement for the soul." Blood atonement means that one life is saved by the sacrificed life of another. It is costly and intensely personal. To think that my life is saved by someone else laying down his life so that I might live is truly stunning. As John 15:13 says, "Greater love has no one than this, than to lay down one's life for his friends." Jesus lays down his life for each one of us personally. It is the ultimate expression of love.

Imagine a mother and a child playing in their front yard. The mother tells the child not to run onto the street because he could be hit by a car. But when the ball rolls into the street, the child excitedly goes after it and does not see the oncoming traffic. The mother sees the car from the porch, runs into the street and pushes the child out of harm's way. In the process she gets hit by the car. This is sacrifice. This is love that almost any good parent can immediately relate to. What parent among us would not do the same for his or her child?

Soldiers can also relate to this kind of sacrifice. I am a conscientious objector, but I am deeply grateful for the willingness of soldiers to go into harm's way in order to keep me free. I have heard soldiers reduced to tears when they tell the stories of how a comrade in arms laid down his life for the sake of his unit or an individual combatant.

I am reminded of the Tom Hanks movie *Saving Private Ryan*. Tom Hanks's character lays down his life to save Private Ryan. All he says as he is dying is, "Go and live a good life." We then fade to a shot of an aged Private Ryan and his family before the gravesite of the captain who gave his life so that he might live. He turns to his elderly wife and tearfully says, "Tell me I have lived a good life." She is reduced to tears as well, as is most of the viewing audience. I know I was!

That is what Jesus does for us. He lays down his life for us that we might live. When we meditate on it we are reduced to tears.

The theology of the atonement is also profound. We believe that Jesus is both human and divine. He is Son of God and Son of Mary. He "bore our sins" (1 Pet 2:24). He paid the price for our redemption and the forgiveness of our sins. We believe he actually bore our sins on the cross. He bore the death that we rightly deserved, for "the wages of sin *is* death" (Rom 6:23).

INCARNATION AND DEIFICATION

God became human in Jesus in order to offer himself as a sacrifice of unimaginable divine love for each of us. In order for Jesus to bear another person's sin he must be a human being "without sin" (Heb 4:15). In order for him to bear more than just one person's sin he must be God, and infinite in his divine nature.

The understanding of the incarnation was at the center of the early church's theological debates that led to the development of central doctrines. Most Christians today routinely accept these creedal teachings as orthodox, but rarely understand the process of their development in the living relationship between sacred Scripture and apostolic tradition. The canon of Scripture as we accept it today, which gives us the first insight into these mysteries about the new covenant knowledge of God through Christ and the Spirit, is a result of that process. Our understanding of the Trinity arose from our understanding of the incarnation of Jesus. The sacramental conception of the Eucharist and teachings about Mary all arose from the salvation experience of the early church, and from the development of our understanding of the mystery of mysteries in the incarnation.

The correct perception of Mary in both the East and the West is essentially tied to maintaining and understanding as much as we can of the mystery of the incarnation, the cross, resurrection and ascension of Jesus, and our participation as his bride in these sacred events in Christ. Jesus is said to be Son of God and Son of Man, and Son of God and Son of Mary. She is not only the *Anthropotokos*, or Mother of Man, but also the *Theotokos*, or Mother of God. Mary is seen not simply as a human incubator, but as a fully human participant in the salvation brought by Jesus. Far too often we have not only thrown the proverbial "baby out with the bathwater" in our approach to the incarnation, but we have also thrown out Jesus' mother, the Theotokos.

The notion that God himself would actually lay down his life for us is overwhelming, not to mention that he subsequently lifts us up to share in his divinity! As Scripture and the Divine Liturgy teach us, he takes on our human nature that we might share in his divinity. The Word became flesh to make us *"partakers of the divine nature"* (2 Pet 1:4). In the second century Irenaeus, bishop of Lyons, said "For this is why the Word became man, and the Son of God became the Son of man: so that man, by entering into communion with the Word and thus receiving divine sonship, might become a son of God." St. Athanasius said, "For the Son of God became man so that we might become God." And St. Thomas Aquinas said much later, "The only-begotten Son of God, wanting to make us sharers in his divinity, assumed our nature, so that he, made man, might make men gods."

In the Christian East this is called "deification" or "theosis," and is an important goal of the Jesus Prayer

THE EUCHARIST

One of the things I loved in the evangelical world, along with its love of Scripture, was its strong belief in Jesus, and the use of the phrase, "a personal love relationship with Jesus Christ." But ironically, I found that many people I encountered still relegated that relationship to mere head knowledge of the Bible. Most could quote book, chapter and verse by memory, but often had an undeveloped understanding of Jesus as a real living person in history, or in their lives today. Despite quoting Scripture to say that grace freed us from the law, many I encountered were still trapped in a rather legal approach to Jesus.

Likewise, many or even most used the language of blood

sacrifice for the atonement, but that remained a very legal term that somehow kept their salvation experience fairly "positional," rather than experiential. This is changing today, but it is still evident when I fellowship in evangelical circles.

For me, the contemplative heritage of the mystics and saints in the more ancient apostolic Catholic, Orthodox and Eastern churches opened that door in a powerful and revelatory way. The Jesus Prayer is part of that heritage. But the Jesus Prayer is always couched within the broader orthodox sacramental experience.

This is especially true of the Eucharist. Eucharist simply means "thanksgiving," and was the word used for the ongoing celebration of the Lord's Supper, or what Catholics more commonly call the Mass (from the Latin *missa*, which simply means "dismissal," for the dismissing of catechumens after the Gospel reading and of the baptized after Communion). Like a tree with deep roots, from its deep sacramental base the more personal practice of the Jesus Prayer could really reach high in the Spirit.

This sacramental tradition involves a full understanding and practice of the Real Presence and sacrifice of Jesus in and through the Eucharist. Even when I first became a Catholic the idea of the Real Presence or sacrifice was still new and developing in me. I accepted it, but on an intuitive level I was still growing into it. I had grown up a good Methodist, had fallen away into the rock 'n' roll culture, and by coming back to Christ through the Jesus Movement of the late '60s and early '70s was steeped in Protestant understanding and practice regarding the Lord's Supper. Now that I am older I find myself being overwhelmed by these more ancient realities of the Eucharist. It is all about the immediacy of the sacrificial love of Jesus for me, and my being personally saved through my personal Savior.

The early church believed that Jesus was mystically truly present in the Eucharist. The belief was not theologically developed, but it was universally accepted, except by those who did not believe that Jesus was either fully God or fully human. The Docetists and early Gnostics in particular abstained from the Eucharist because if a person did not accept the fullness of the incarnation, it made no sense to believe in the Son's continued sacramental incarnation in the Eucharist. In other words, if the Logos did not fully embrace flesh and blood, the notion of Jesus being fully but mystically present in the Eucharist made no sense. The Eucharist was the early church's way of affirming the incarnation of the Logos in Jesus, body and blood, soul and divinity, sacramentally at every Eucharist. It was affirmed beyond mere human understanding or words by the simple *act* of the sacrament. It is a silent but most powerful proclamation of the Word by the simple act of being.

In his *Letter to the Smyrnaeans* St. Ignatius of Antioch said,

Take note of those who hold heterodox opinions on the grace of Jesus Christ which has come to us, and see how contrary their opinions are to the mind of God. . . .

They abstain from the Eucharist and from prayer because they do not confess that the Eucharist is the flesh of our Savior Jesus Christ, flesh which suffered for our sins and which that Father, in his goodness, raised up again. They who deny the gift of God are perishing in their disputes.

The early church also believed in the sacrificial character of the Eucharist. In his letter to the Corinthians, Clement of Rome said, "Our sin will not be small if we eject from the episcopate those who blamelessly and holily have offered its sacrifices." Ignatius of Antioch, in his letter to the Philadelphians, said,

Make certain, therefore, that you all observe one common Eucharist; for there is but one body of our Lord Jesus Christ, and but one cup of union with his blood, and one single altar of sacrifice—even as there is also but one bishop, with his clergy and my own fellow servitors, the deacons. This will ensure that all your doings are in full accord with the will of God.

This also affects our understanding of sacramental sacrifice today. Jesus gave his life for us two thousand years ago on Calvary. He died that we might live. He shed his blood "once for all" (Heb 7:27; 9:12). But the Orthodox and Catholics believe that he is present and gives his life "sacramentally" or through "sacred mystery," extended and repeated in an "unbloody" sacrifice every day in the Eucharist. (The early church and even the first Protestant Reformers believed in the Real Presence and sacrifice as well, though they theologically adapted it in various ways.) Jesus is fully present in the Eucharist in a way that is frankly beyond our understanding.

This means that sacramentally Jesus is timelessly giving his very life for us daily and at every moment. The reality of his final sacrifice on Calvary is brought into the present moment at every Eucharist. This is most powerful for the one who understands it. The Real Presence and sacrifice of Jesus are brought right into our daily experience as a sacramental act, not as a mere theology from the past. There is simply no way to meditate on this reality and not be filled with tearful gratitude for Jesus giving his life for us. If we understand this, there is simply no way to receive Communion without being overwhelmed as well. Salvation becomes an immediate reality that reduces us to tears and lifts us up to joy!

I find the Eucharist a powerful way to experience daily the sacrifice of Jesus for me personally. This happens not through mere theology or intellectual understanding. It occurs in a simple sacramental act of the Logos, which is beyond human words. It is an action that reduces me to sacred stillness, *hesychia*.

Do we allow ourselves to sink into the mystery of salvation, or do we skim across the surface of the waters of salvation with a mere intellectual understanding? Jesus is our Savior. How can we but not weep tears of gratitude, repentance and pure joy when we meditate on him?

Every time we pray the Jesus Prayer we enter into the daily reality of our salvation in the Savior in a way that lies beyond words. It must be a prayer. It must be breathed. It must be in in the Spirit of Jesus, our Savior, and author of our personal salvation.

PRACTICE

As we breathe in, let's allow the salvation that only Jesus can bring to fill us up. Allow it to be personal and intimate. We breathe in the reality of Jesus' personal sacrifice for "me," personally. Allow this sacrifice to be personal and now, not a mere theological idea from the past, but *now*. Jesus loves you enough to give his life for you out of complete self-emptying love. We allow Jesus to transform us moment by moment with each breath we breathe!

3

Christicket

Lord, Jesus *Christ* . . .

*T*he next word in the Jesus Prayer is *Christ*, which means "anointed." It comes from the Greek *Christos*. It was used for the Messiah and applied to Jesus as the "anointed One"— Christ. As followers of Jesus we are called Christians. This comes from Acts 11:26, where this name was given to followers of Jesus in Antioch by others outside of the faith, and 1 Peter 4:16, where it is related to both self-identity and enduring sufferings with Christ. Some have said that it means "like Christ."

We are to be anointed like Christ (2 Cor 1:21). The word for "anointed" here is the Greek *chriō*, which is probably akin to *chraomai*, meaning "to make ready for use" through being "rubbed or smeared with oil" or to be consecrated to an office or religious service. It is used to consecrate Jesus to the messianic office, furnishing him with the necessary powers to give Christians the gifts of the Holy Spirit. Our anointing is not a right as it is for the incarnate Logos (Word), the second person of the Trinity, but is a gift bestowed on us as the adopted sons and daughters of God in Christ (Rom 8:15). Our anointing comes from and leads back to Christ Jesus.

ANOINTED BY THE SPIRIT

I came back to Christ through the Jesus Movement, albeit through a side door of interfaith studies! The Jesus Movement was largely Pentecostal and charismatic, so when I became a Catholic I naturally sought out the Catholic Charismatic Renewal. (I also encountered the Evangelical Orthodox Church in Indianapolis, a charismatic expression of the Orthodox tradition, using the Liturgy of St. John Chrysostom in their worship.) Though rather hidden in small groups in most parishes in America at that time, Catholic Charismatics still constituted the largest single united body of charismatics in the world. I found them everywhere.

I fondly remember my first encounters with them even before I became Catholic; they welcomed me to prayer meetings and charismatic Masses. How well I remember the sweet Spirit-filled encounters with Catholics at the old Alverna Franciscan Retreat Center, where I found my Catholic vocation, or the wonderful Tuesday night prayer meetings at Marian College in Indianapolis. I met friends in the Spirit who nurtured me in the beginnings of my Catholic faith and are still dear friends today.

I also recall Father Paulson at the old Charismatic Center in Houston asking me to play at a Mass during my Jesus music days. I replied that I didn't even know what a Mass was! He said in a unique Texas drawl, "Ya love Jesus don't ya?" I said yes! So he warmly welcomed me as a brother in Christ and allowed me to play at the Preparation of the Gifts after the Intercessions and before the formal Liturgy of the Eucharist, though I was not yet a Catholic or ready to receive the Eucharist at that stage in my spiritual journey. His kindness stays with me to this day.

ENTHUSIASM IN THE SPIRIT

But Father Paulson, like most leaders in the Renewal, was also a practical guy. He was well aware that sometimes charismatics are really just charismaniacs! Sometimes we Catholic Charismatics think we're anointed but we're only excited! There is a huge difference. You can get excited about a football game, but it doesn't mean that the Spirit of God anoints you. You can even get excited about Jesus and miss the real anointing of the Spirit of Jesus. I remember all too well a plaque on the wall of the pastor's study at the Warehouse Ministry in Sacramento, California: "We want spiritual fruit, not religious nuts!" Amen!

This leads us to the notion of religious enthusiasm. *Enthusiasm* means to be *en theos* or "in God" (from the Greek *entheos*, "divinely inspired," "possessed by a god").

John Wesley once wrote a sermon and tract on enthusiasm because he had seen so many religious extremists around his ministry. Enthusiasm had a negative connotation in his day. Both he and his associate John Whitefield were under suspicion because they preached of the power of the Holy Spirit and attracted enthusiastic people to their meetings. In fact, John Wesley was internally conflicted at times regarding the power of the Spirit he encountered among the more mystical Moravians, whom he befriended, and in phenomenon of the Spirit he personally experienced while ministering to large crowds. Wesley felt a need to explain himself through a sermon that balanced legitimate enthusiasm against mere religious fanaticism.

At Little Portion Monastery and in JMT Itinerant Ministry we also encounter religious fanatics. The *Didache*, or *The Teaching of the Twelve Apostles*, an early church writing, calls fanaticism a sin. It says, "Never give way to anger, for anger leads to homicide. Likewise refrain from fanaticism, quarrelling, and hot-temperedness, for these too can breed homicide."

There is a big difference between fanatics and radicals. Radicals (from the Latin *radix*, "root," and *radicalis*, "of roots") are like radishes, which are "rooted." Fanatics simply mimic certain externals of genuine radicalism without understanding the roots and spirituality behind the religious practice. They often degenerate into emotional legalists and are almost always destructive. But the word *fanatic* (Latin, *fanaticus*, "inspired by a deity, frenzied," which comes from *fanum*, "temple") is similar to the origin of *enthusiastic*, and cautions us about the negative aspect of false religious enthusiasm.

The Rule of St. Benedict speaks of Sarabaites and Gyrovagues as unstable religious people. We have already encountered two good kinds of monks. Now let's examine two bad kinds. Of them the Rule says in chapter one:

> Third, there are the Sarabaites, the most detestable kind of monks, who with no experience to guide them, no rule to try them as gold is tried in a furnace (Prov. 27:21), have a character as soft as lead. Still loyal to the world by their actions, they clearly lie to God by their tonsure. Two or three together, or even alone, without a shepherd, they pen themselves up in their own sheepfolds, not the Lord's. Their law is what they like to do, whatever strikes their fancy. Anything they believe in and choose, they call holy; anything they dislike, they consider forbidden. Fourth and finally, there are the monks called gyrovagues, who spend their entire lives drifting from region to region, staying as guests for three or four days in different monasteries. Always on the move, they never settle down, and are slaves to their own wills and gross appetites. In every way they are worse than the sarabaites.

"We want spiritual fruit, not religious nuts!" Only when couched in correct understanding can the contemplative experience of the Prayer not drift off into illusion that even ends in delusion.

TABORIC LIGHT

The Spirit had been poured forth on the early church at Pentecost, but in a way that brought forth radical change for the better in their lives as a renewed community. The Spirit is the power of Jesus that made him more than a typical religious founder or a good religious idea. Through the Spirit we have a personal encounter with the full incarnation of God in Christ (Acts 2). Jesus said, "Behold, I send the Promise of My Father upon you; but tarry in the city of Jerusalem until you are endued with power from on high" (Lk 24:49). The Greek word for "power" is *dynamis*, which is the origin of our word *dynamite*. But dynamite can be used for good or ill (for example, blowing up bank vaults or clearing away rock for highways)! So St. Paul had to write to correct the abuses of that power by the Corinthians (1 Cor 12–14).

Hesychasm (meaning "sacred stillness"), an ancient practice of hermits in the Eastern Church, focuses on the actual experience of the Spirit of God. One Hesychast was St. Seraphim of Sarov (1754 or 1759–1833), sometimes called "The St. Francis of Russia," who became well-known through the book *The Acquisition of the Holy Spirit*. It records the following interaction: "Then Father Seraphim gripped me firmly by the shoulders and said: 'My friend, both of us, at this moment are in the Holy Spirit, you and I. Why won't you look at me?'

'I can't look at you, Father, because the light flashing from your eyes and face is brighter than the sun and I'm dazzled!'

'Don't be afraid, friend of God, you yourself are shining just like I am; you too are now in the fullness of grace of the Holy Spirit, otherwise you wouldn't be able to see me as you do.'"

Hesychasts like St. Gregory Palamas (1296–1359) differentiated between the uncreated energies and the essence of God. The phenomenon of the Spirit, or any knowable aspect of God in the phenomenal world, is part of God's uncreated energies, which emanate from him. In contrast, God's essence is part of God's transcendence, and so is beyond human perception through any knowable faculty. At best the essence of God can be intuited in contemplative union that is sometimes called "unknowing."

The Hesychasts were criticized, not for their belief in the essence of God, but for their experiences of the supernatural gifts of the Spirit. Ever since the Montanist heresy of the second century, the entire church had been rather leery of trusting in charismatic gifts. Indeed, the Montanists trusted in the gifts over the apostolic authority of the bishops, and this ended up in schism and heresy.

Ironically, the Hesychasts, who were known for "sacred stillness" and contemplation, had to verbally defend their position on their experience of the supernatural phenomenon! In his famous fourteenth-century answer to Barlaam of Calabria, a Westerner who taught that God is transcendent beyond any human experiences, St. Gregory Palamas used his explanation of God's knowable uncreated energies to defend the Hesychasts. Until recently the West has continued to resist this teaching on Western patristic grounds. But this has changed, particularly since John Paul II praised Hesychasm and the Christian East for its mystical heights.

The phenomenon the Hesychasts experienced was called Taboric Light (also Uncreated Light and Divine Light). It is the light experienced by Jesus on the Mount of Transfiguration, traditionally held to be Mount Tabor in lower Galilee of the Holy Land. There, Jesus was transfigured with light, conversed with Moses and Elijah about his passion and glorification, and is overshadowed by a cloud, during which a voice said, "This is My beloved Son. Hear Him!" These were all perceptible by the apostles but were clearly outside of the natural phenomenon of ordinary existence. When the cloud subsided "Jesus was found alone" (Lk 9:28-36). Such phenomenon are considered Uncreated Energies. They are part of the spiritual journey to a contemplative place—complete intuitive communion—beyond understanding or description. It simply must be experienced to be understood.

So, the phenomenon of the gift of the Spirit has been controversial to say the least. Catholics and evangelicals took quite a bit of time to accept the Charismatic Renewal, and some still do not. But under various names these phenomenon have accompanied the saints of the East and the West throughout our history. The dialogue between the Christian East and West continues regarding Hesychasm, but great headway is being made on a popular (and even a theological) level. The greatest test of the authenticity of all such phenomenon of the Spirit is always seen in whether they make us more like Jesus or lead us to delusion through pride.

LIKE JESUS

A great way to ensure that we are really anointed is to transfer the meaning of *Christian*, or like Christ, to like Jesus. In other words, put some flesh and blood on the anointing! Let the anointing of the Spirit be incarnational, just as Jesus was the incarnate Word. What does it mean to be anointed by the Spirit "like Jesus"? A few key Scriptures point the way: the Sermon on the Mount, 1 Corinthians 13, the fruit of the Spirit in Galatians 5:22, and the great canticle of self-emptying love, Philippians 2:5-11.

God is love (1 Jn 4:8), and love fulfills the law of God (Rom 13:8). St. Augustine, the great theologian of divine love, said, "Love, and do what you will." But what is love?

There are three Greek words for love, the social or unconditional agape *(agapaō)*, the affection of friendship in phileo *(phileō)*, and the passion of eros *(erōs)*. The first two are primarily found in the New Testament, but all three were used in the early church. While often relegated to an inferior kind of love, eros can be the positive passionate lifting of ourselves above ourselves by loving. Pope Benedict XVI relates the gift of all three in his encyclical "God Is Love." The main characteristic of all three forms of love is self-giving or self-emptying for the sake of another. The greatest "other" is God and neighbor.

St. Paul also writes rapturously of love in the great love chapter of 1 Corinthians 13. He says, "Love is patient, love is kind. It is not jealous, (love) is not pompous, it is not inflated, it is not rude, it does not seek its own interests [Greek, literally "seek itself"], it is not quick-tempered. . . . Love never fails" (1 Cor 13:4-5, 8 RNAB).

This description could well apply to Jesus! In the early days of the Jesus Movement we were encouraged to substitute the name of Jesus for *love*. If we are like Jesus, we can put our name there as well. Such a meditation will surely begin to change us, moving us from the mind of meditation to the emotions and actions of our entire life. It will help us become more like Christ.

We know that the fruit of the Spirit is similar. The Greek word for "spirit" is *pneuma*, meaning "air," "wind" and "breath." It can apply to both the Holy Spirit and the human spirit. The "fruit of the Spirit" has been translated both ways, for both bring forth good fruit when they are the primary mode of operation in our lives if we are operating in the Spirit of God.

What are the fruits of the Spirit?

Galatians 5:22-25 lists them as "love, joy, peace, patience, kindness, generosity, faithfulness, gentleness, self-control. Against such there is no law. Now those who belong to Christ [Jesus] have crucified their flesh with its passions and desires. If we live by the Spirit, let us also follow the Spirit" (RNAB).

Who does not want to live like this? It is the deepest desire of every human being, whether we are aware of it or not. As Augustine said, "My heart is restless until it rests in You." We all want the victory of love over hate, joy over sorrow and despair, peace over conflict and war, patience over impatience, kindness over cruelty, generosity over consumerism, faithfulness over destructive doubt, gentleness over arrogance and pride, and self-control over unbridled promiscuity. Jesus shows us the way to such beauty that every human heart longs for.

But Paul's description also shows us the mechanics of how to get there. "Those who belong to Christ Jesus have crucified their flesh with its passions and desires. If we live by the Spirit, let us also follow the Spirit." This is a mouthful! But it is not complicated. The way to the release of the Spirit of God, and the rebirth of our deepest spirit and truest self, is through the dying and rising of Jesus, not just as an idea but also as an experience! The Jesus Prayer is one prayer aid that will actually get us there.

The last Scripture that reveals to us the character of being like Jesus is St. Paul's letter to the Philippians. In chapter 2 he says,

> Though he was in the form of God,
> [Jesus] did not regard equality with God something to
>   be grasped.
> Rather, he emptied himself,
> taking the form of a slave,
> coming in human likeness,
> and found human in appearance,
> he humbled himself,
> becoming obedient to death, even death on a cross.
> Because of this, God greatly exalted him
> and bestowed on him the name
> that is above every name,
> that at the name of Jesus
> every knee should bend,
> of those in heaven and on earth and under the earth,
> and every tongue confess that
> Jesus Christ is Lord,
> to the glory of God the Father. (Phil 2:6-11 RNAB)

This is the Scripture describing better than any other the self-emptying or kenosis (from the Greek *kenos*, meaning "to empty oneself completely") of Jesus. This is found in the incarnation of the divine Logos as a human being, the second person of the Trinity, who is eternally begotten from the Father in the Godhead. But it reaches its climax in the mystery of mysteries—the paschal mystery of the cross. Only because of this did God the Father give him the name above every name and a glory above all others.

We can now share in this mystery as we become like Jesus Christ as Christians and catholics. We can share in the *katholikos* of being abundantly and universally filled with the anointing of Jesus Christ! It is what we all hunger for. It is only when we experience this that we will find the love, joy and peace of the spirit that only the Spirit of God can bring through dying and rising to our old selves once and for all.

CATHOLIC

It is interesting that the city where the name Christian was first used was also the city of St. Ignatius of Antioch (first century), who first used the word *catholic* (*katholikos* in Greek), which means "universal and full," and has both ecclesial and personal ramifications. It addresses church structure and personal piety. Later, we will look to the more personal and ecumenical aspects, but a few more ecclesial sources will help us to understand how important proper church life was to the early Hesychasts.

In his *Letter to the Smyrnaeans* Ignatius says, "Wherever the bishop appears, there let the people be; as wherever Jesus Christ is, there is the Catholic Church. It is not lawful to baptize or give communion without the consent of the bishop."

St. Vincent of Lérins, on a monastic island off the southern coast of Gaul, wrote in 434 a work known as the *Commoni-*

toria. In it he addressed a question that some were asking about the authority of the church:

> Since the canon of Scripture is complete, and sufficient of itself for everything, and more than sufficient, what need is there to join with it the authority of the Church's interpretation? For this reason,—because, owing to the depth of Holy Scripture, all do not accept it in one and the same sense, but one understands its words in one way, another in another. . . . Therefore, it is very necessary, on account of so great intricacies of such various error, that the rule for the right understanding of the prophets and apostles should be framed in accordance with the standard of Ecclesiastical and Catholic interpretation.

While he insisted that, like the human body, church doctrine develops while truly keeping its identity, St. Vincent further declared that in the Catholic Church: "we hold that faith which has been believed everywhere, always, by all. For that is truly and in the strictest sense 'catholic.'" This statement has become a standard description of the Catholic faith. Of course, this must be nuanced by Vincent's other notion of development of doctrine that was expounded and expanded so beautifully with the great John Henry Newman (1801–1890) in Britain. St. Vincent wrote, "But some one will say, perhaps, Shall there, then, be no progress in Christ's Church? Certainly; all possible progress. . . . Yet on condition that it be real progress, not alteration of the faith."

Development of doctrine is not some lifeless concept, but based on the reality of life itself. It maintains that the acorn and the oak are essentially the same tree, but only seen at different stages of growth. Likewise, a stream takes on many different appearances as it faces different obstacles and landscapes at different stages of its journey to the sea, but it is essentially the same water throughout. The same is true of doctrine. The incarnation, the Trinity, the Eucharist and all truths remain constant, but our understanding develops as we face various obstacles and questions at various stages of the growth of the church in history. This is a life-giving principle.

Scripture itself teaches us that we are living stones in a spiritual temple built on the foundation of the apostles and the prophets with Christ Jesus as the cornerstone. We must build squarely on what has come before, neither leaning to the right nor the left. But we must, to paraphrase *Star Trek,* place our stone in space "where no stone has gone before!" This is both conserving of the apostolic tradition of the past, and progressive in applying it today as we move into the future. This is exciting, and most life giving, and is essential in being truly catholic and full.

The term *catholic* means that Jesus is found in us universally and fully, from head to toe, from the inside out, and from the outside in. We must be transformed into Jesus Christ. For me, whether in the Roman Catholic heritage or elsewhere, that essential change in the substance of our being remains the greatest fruit of a genuine Christian faith. We must become Christian and catholic. We must be anointed by the Spirit, like Jesus and like Christ. To be fully anointed, we love as fully as possible in this life, or universally like Christ. That is the meaning of the word *catholic*. To be catholic is the fulfillment of the abundance and fullness promised by Christ himself in John 10.

This is at least some of what we mean when we pray "Lord, Jesus Christ" in the context of the Jesus Prayer.

PRACTICE

As we breathe in we allow ourselves to be universally and completely filled with the real person of Jesus through the Holy Spirit. Love, joy, peace and all the fruit of the Spirit transform us from the inside out—spirit, soul and body. As an intuition of our spirit in his Spirit, we allow him to transform our thoughts, emotions and actions. With every breath we are completely and abundantly transformed into being like Christ, Christian and fully catholic through and through! It also breaks down the barriers of arrogance and pride that stand between us and everyone else in the church, our families and the entire human family. We become fully catholic!

4

Son of God,
Part 1

Lord, Jesus Christ, *Son of God* . . .

*T*he next words of the Jesus Prayer are a term that forms a complete reality: "Son of God." These words are simple, but far from simplistic. Implied in these three words is the very heart of the orthodox understanding of the Christian faith: The Trinity and the incarnation, not to mention the church and the sacraments, especially the Eucharist.

There is nothing particularly significant in the Greek language regarding the meaning of the words themselves. The word for "son" is *huios*, which means exactly what it does in English!

The word for "God" is *theos*, and is the root for words like *theology* (the study of God) and *theosis* (the notion of deification so important to Hesychasm). In Greek *theos* can be applied to gods or even to human leaders as God's representatives.

In the Jewish Scriptures there is a "Son of God" who walks with the three young men in Nebuchadnezzar's fiery furnace. "'Look!' he answered, 'I see four men loose, walking in the midst of the fire; and they are not hurt, and the form of the fourth is like the Son of God'" (Dan 3:25). Christians consider this to be a preincarnational appearance of the Son of God.

These words were not formally included in the Jesus Prayer until Nicephoros, an Athonite monk of the Holy Mountain around 1340, added it. In his work, *Guarding the Heart*, he says, "Take away all discursive thought from the reason . . . and give it to the invocation, 'Lord Jesus Christ, Son of God, have mercy on me.'" This exhibits the fluidity of the development of the Jesus Prayer. Such developments are important and should not be jettisoned just because they appear later. This is not unlike the development of Christian doctrine itself.

CULTURAL SIGNIFICANCE

But the term *Son of God* has rather surprising cultural and even political significance. The term was used also of the Caesars in the Roman Empire. Emperors and rulers ranging from China to Japan to Alexander the Great (c. 356–323 B.C.) have assumed titles that reflect a filial relationship with deities. Around the time of Jesus the title *divi filius* (son of the divine one) was associated with Emperor Augustus (as adopted son of Julius Caesar). Later, it was also used to refer to Domitian, the son of Vespasian. Augustus used the title as well.

The title "Son of God" has dramatic significance on the Christian use of the term. Not only was it a theological description, it was also cultural and even political! It reached out to folks of the day with language they all understood. When people referred to Jesus as the "Son of God," it meant that he, and not Caesar, was the ultimate authority in heaven and on earth.

For Christians this term also implies that Jesus is the incarnation of the Logos, the second person of the Trinity.

THE TRINITY

Both the Trinity and the incarnation are clearly found in Scripture, but not in more developed forms. It took Christians, and specifically the church, to grapple with the subtleties of these mysteries and develop language about them that is relevant, balanced and true. But because we admit that we are stating mysteries that defy full human description, the development of these Christian doctrines continues today.

I am reminded of the quaint story of St. Augustine told to countless Catholic school children (and to me by my spiritual father!). Bishop Augustine was preaching his series of homilies on the Trinity in the cathedral in Hippo. Between services he would walk the seashore to meditate and rest his

mind. He saw a boy on the shore digging a hole and then
filling the hole with a bucket of seawater. He did this repeatedly. Finally Augustine walked over to the boy and asked,
"Son, what are you doing?" The boy replied, "I am going to
take that big ocean and put it in this little hole." The wise and
fatherly Bishop Augustine said kindly to the boy, "My son,
that ocean is too big to place in that little hole." The boy
looked up at the bishop, and said, "Easier for me to take that
big ocean and put it in this little hole than for you to take the
big Trinity and put it in your little mind, Bishop Augustine!"
At that the boy disappeared. He was an angel sent by God to
remind Augustine that sublime as his teaching might be, he
could never fully understand or express the divine mysteries
of the Trinity (or the incarnation, for that matter).

Many people hear the words *Son of God* and immediately
think of the incarnation of the Word in Jesus through the
Virgin Mary. We immediately see the manger and hear the
angels singing and such. But the term really applies more
fundamentally to the Trinity.

The English translation of the Latin version of the Nicene
Creed says,

> I *believe* in one Lord Jesus Christ,
> the only-*begotten* Son of God,
> *born* of the Father *before all ages*.
>
> God from God, Light from Light,
> true God from true God,

begotten, not made,
consubstantial with the Father. (The New Roman
    Missal, 3rd edition; emphasis added)

St. Bonaventure teaches on the mystery of the Trinity most beautifully. Ewert Cousins's book *The Coincidence of Opposites* in the Bonaventure series by the old Franciscan Herald Press was really the first book that got through to me on the beauty and balance of the Trinity. Though he wrote masterfully on the paradoxes of the Trinity, he also presented the teaching of Bonaventure in a way that made sense. The logic goes like this:

God is one and utterly transcendent and self-sufficient. He is the I AM, YHWH, "the existent one" or "underived existence." But God is also goodness and love. Goodness is self-diffusive, meaning he pours himself out freely, which implies someone other must be there to receive from God. Of course, this is the Son. This is why God is often spoken of as both plural and neuter under the ancient title of *'ĕlōhîm* or Elohim in Hebrew. God is also love (1 Jn 4:8). Love is the self-emptying union of two to generate at least one other, or a third.

Many would say that God creates out of his goodness and love, which emanates into creation. But we should not say that God "must" create in order to satisfy his goodness and love, which would mean that God is no longer self-sufficient. Though God is love, which emanates from him, he always remains self-sufficient and transcendent.

So, God is self-sufficient or self-enclosed. Yet, if the one God is goodness and love and self-diffusive, he must be plural, triune—Father, Son and Holy Spirit. Since God is timeless, or eternal, this triune reality exists without beginning or end. The Son of God is eternally begotten of the Father within the mystery of the Trinity even now, and will be without end.

In the early fourteenth century in the Christian East, a bishop of ancient Philadelphia put this into rather decisive trinitarian language. He divides the human person into *nous* (spiritual mind), *logos* (word) and *pneuma* (spirit). *Logos* has a clear connection to the Son of God, and *pneuma* to the Holy Spirit. He says, "Pure prayer unites in itself the nous, the logos, and the pneuma. Through the logos it invokes God's name. Through the nous it calmly fixes its gaze on the God whom it invokes. Through the pneuma it manifests compunction, humility and love. In this way it calls upon the eternal Trinity, Father, Son, and Holy Spirit, the one and only God."

St. Bonaventure uses a similar technique in the West. He says that human person is "memory, intellect, and will," which leads us to the Trinity. Memory leads to time and timelessness into God and eternity. Intellect leads to divine truth. And will is the seat of love, and leads us to God's love.

St. Paul uses "spirit, soul, and body" (1 Thess 5:23). I have used this with a more modern incorporation of Eastern understandings. Spirit means intuition beyond ideas, forms and words in pure contemplation. Soul is spiritual mind and means meditation. Body means senses, emotions and intellectual thought.

Spirit, soul and body, and their corresponding contemplative prayer, meditation and asceticism, are at best human tools to help us understand the divine mystery of the Trinity. The human person remains an integrated whole that defies strict classifications into parts. But such classifications, though not absolute, help us understand ourselves better. The same could certainly be said of the Trinity. Though these doctrines are true, they never grasp the full mystery, which lies beyond our complete understanding. In fact, I suspect that after this life we will be awed by God's presence, and will see how little we actually understood.

The second person of the Trinity is the Logos, or Word of the Father. The early church struggled with how this all worked. The preexistence and eternal begottenness of the Logos were neither instantly believed nor fully understood. Some believed that the Word came into being when he was born on earth. Others believed he was in the mind of God eternally, but was only begotten at some point before creation. Through prayerful and sometimes aggressive dialogue and debate over a few hundred years, well-intentioned, spiritual and intelligent bishops and theologians hammered out the understanding of the Trinity that orthodox Christians accept today.

The word *consubstantial* ("consubstantial with the Father") was in the first English translation of the Latin version of the Creed, has been retained in many traditions, and was re-introduced into the current edition of the Catholic Mass (Roman Missal, third edition). It means "of one substance" and refers to the Son's relation to the Father. The Greek is *homoousios* (from the Ancient Greek *homos*, "same," and *ousia*, "essence, being") and is often translated "one in essence" in the Eastern versions of the Nicene Creed.

While not directly related to "Son of God" in the Jesus Prayer, the place of the Holy Spirit in the Trinity does warrant some comment. The person of the Spirit was not seriously considered until such works as *On the Holy Spirit* by St. Basil the Great (329/330–379) were written. Before the church fathers could fully consider the Spirit, they had to establish the Son's relation to the Father. Up to this point, many thought the Holy Spirit was the preexistent form of the Logos. Others believed the Holy Spirit was the power of the Father emanating into creation to accomplish his will and to anoint leaders and prophets.

I must admit that I probably shared this latter view in the early days of my return to Christianity within the Jesus Movement, though I intellectually would have adhered to the orthodox teaching regarding the place of the Spirit in the Trinity. It was only as I discovered the wonders of patristics that my view was broadened, balanced and catapulted into the wonders of paradox in God.

The Roman Catholic version of the Nicene Creed says:

I believe in the Holy Spirit,
the Lord, the giver of life,
who proceeds from the Father and the Son,
who with the Father and the Son
is adored and glorified,
who has spoken through the prophets.
(Emphasis added)

The words *and the Son* were added in the Latin translation of the Creed. The original Greek version of the Nicene Creed, to which the Orthodox Church holds and which it still in the Greek Version of the Creed even in the Roman West, says:

And [we believe] in the Holy Spirit, the Lord, the Giver of Life, who proceeds from the Father; who with the Father and the Son together is worshipped and glorified; who spoke by the prophets.

The Christian East holds the original Nicene Creed position that the Son is eternally begotten of the Father and the Spirit eternally proceeds solely from the Father. The West was facing a different set of Christological controversies that necessitated an emphasis on the second person of the Trinity. Thus the Western church emphasized that the Spirit eternally proceeds from the Father *and* the Son. Augustine beautifully stated that the eternal procession of the Spirit is from the love union with the Father and the Son. The problem from the

Eastern perspective is that this places an imbalance in the inner workings of the Trinity. Nevertheless, the West felt biblically justified by the Scriptures that imply that the Son sends the Spirit from the Father.

As a Roman Catholic I must confess that my *mind* sides with the logic of the East on this one. But the beauty of love in the Trinity as described by St. Augustine inspires my *heart*. In the end, Scripture is determinative and brings me down, albeit with hesitance, on the side of the Latin West.

Texts such as John 20:22 ("He breathed on *them* and said to them, 'Receive the Holy Spirit'") were seen by some of the church fathers, especially Athanasius, Cyril of Alexandria and Epiphanius of Cyprus, as proofs that the Spirit "proceeds substantially from both" the Father and the Son. Other texts that have been used include Galatians 4:6, Romans 8:9, Philippians 1:19, where the Holy Spirit is called "the Spirit of His Son," "the Spirit of Christ" and "the Spirit of Jesus Christ." Of course, the Gospel of John speaks clearly of Jesus sending the Holy Spirit.

As we can see, the spirituality and history of the Trinity is rich and deep. The Trinity is simply intuited when we repeat the Jesus Prayer's words *Son of God*. But understanding the basics helps to keep that intuition from falling into illusion.

So, when we pray "Son of God" in the Jesus Prayer, we are implying an entire mystical theology of the Trinity. It is wonderfully balanced logic *and* utterly beyond our complete comprehension all at once. This paradox inspires awe and wonder before the timeless mystery of God.

PRACTICE

With this section of the Jesus Prayer we breathe in the fullness of the mystery of the Trinity. We breathe in the unity and diversity of persons in our nuclear families and in the church. We also breathe in the mystery of mysteries, the paradoxes of our faith and life on earth as it is in heaven. We allow ourselves to be changed in our very essence and substance through Jesus. This happens not merely as an idea but as a living reality with every breath.

5

Son of God,
Part 2

Lord, Jesus Christ, *Son of God* . . .

INCARNATION

The deeper meaning of the words *Son of God* does not stop
with the Trinity. The mystery of the Trinity is incarnate in
time and space.

The incarnation of the Word is hinted at in the Jewish tradition with the emanation of God through creation and salvation history. Other religions similarly teach of God or the
gods immanence within creation. These writings often
contain much of the wonder, beauty, truth and the love of

God. This is humanity reaching out to God. But God also reaches back in what we call "revelation." God revealed himself to the Jewish people in a special and intentional way, which is represented in their life, Scriptures and worship.

Christians believe that with Jesus God revealed himself in flesh. We no longer believe merely in the Word on tablets of stone but in a living and incarnate Word—the human being Jesus Christ. We are a people *with* a book, not a people *of* the book. We do not believe in a book but in the living Word, Jesus, the Word made flesh.

I once met a fellow at a Jesus festival outside of Chicago in the early years of Jesus music. I was becoming Catholic and was radically rethinking the notion of *sola scriptura* (Scripture alone) as understood and practiced by many American Protestants. He said, "My life was a mess until I came into a personal love relationship with the Bible!" I must admit that I was stunned by his statement, and most Protestants I tell this story to are stunned as well! I thought to myself how sad this was, and while I was glad that he loved the Scriptures, he was committing a sort of idolatry in the name of Jesus by making the Scriptures more important than Jesus!

And regarding Christ's church, St. Paul says, "You are our letter, written on our hearts, known and read by all, shown to be a letter of Christ administered by us, written not in ink but by the Spirit of the living God, not on tablets of stone but on tablets that are hearts of flesh" (2 Cor 3:2-3 RNAB).

THE INCARNATE SON

Jesus is not just a son of God. He is the "only begotten" Son of God (1 Jn 4:9). The Greek word is *monogenēs*, meaning "sole or only born child." The root of this word is *monos*, from which we get the word *monk*, which means "one" and "alone." *Monogenēs* is applied to Jesus in the New Testament.

This places Christianity outside the comfort zone of many practitioners of other faiths. The Romans and Greeks would perhaps consider adding Jesus to their pantheon of gods, but his exclusive claim to be *the* Son of God set him at odds with their existing deities (and with the Roman emperors themselves). I experienced much the same thing in India. While most Hindus are ready to accept Jesus as another avatar of the Brahman, the Absolute Spirit of the One, they will not consider him to be the "only begotten" Son of God.

We believe that Jesus is fully human *and* fully divine. Most of the early church struggled to find this balance. The Docetists and Gnostics believed that Jesus was fully divine, but not fully human. The Judaizers, Ebionites and Arians believed that he was fully human, but not fully divine. Some believed that the incarnation of the Logos took place at Jesus' baptism after he proved himself obedient though the temptation in the desert. Others believed that the incarnation took place at his birth. The Catholic, Orthodox and most of the Protestant community believes the incarnation took place at Jesus' conception.

The Nicene Creed says:

For us men and for our salvation
he came down from heaven,
and by the Holy Spirit
was incarnate of the Virgin Mary, and became man.
(Emphasis added)

This is stunning! The second person of the Trinity became a human being, incarnate in the womb of the Virgin Mary—too much for the human mind to take in. But Jesus was not some ghost or theophany (*theophaneia*, meaning "appearance of God"), a divine disclosure in the appearance of an angel, a human or an inanimate form. The word *incarnate* literally means "in meat or flesh." At a Mexican restaurant, when we want red meat, we order *carne*. Jesus is the Word "in carne." He was the full, red-blooded incarnation of the Logos!

As John's Gospel says so clearly, "In the beginning was the Word, and the Word was with God, and the Word was God. He was in the beginning with God. . . . And the Word became flesh and dwelt among us, and we beheld His glory, the glory as of the only begotten of the Father, full of grace and truth" (Jn 1:1-14). As 1 John says, "That which was from the beginning, which we have heard, which we have seen with our eyes, which we have looked upon, and our hands have handled, concerning the Word of life" (1 Jn 1:1).

The first five centuries of the church were an intense period of development in our understanding of the incar-

nation. Beyond the heterodox theories mentioned above, the
Nestorians denied the full divinity and humanity in the one
person of Jesus Christ. Apollinarians believed Christ's human
spirit and soul were absorbed in his divinity. Monophysites
tried to express the incarnation as occurring in one nature,
while the mainline church insisted on human and divine natures in the one Christ. This also affected the understandings
of his human will and knowledge.

In his *Enchiridion* St. Augustine said,

> So Christ Jesus, the Son of God, is God and man: God
> before all worlds, man in our world. . . . Therefore, in-
> sofar as he is God, he and the Father are one, and insofar
> as he is man, the Father is greater than he. . . . And
> through this he was both made less and remained equal,
> one and the same person in each case, as has been said.
> But he is different as regards the Word and as regards
> man: as regards the Word he is equal, as regards man
> lesser; one and the same person is Son of Man and Son of
> God; there are not two sons of God, divine and human,
> but one Son of God, God without beginning, man from a
> certain beginning in time, our Lord Jesus Christ.

The Catechism of the Catholic Church summarizes in a
way that most orthodox Christians heartily echo:

III. *True God and True Man*

464 The unique and altogether singular event of the

Incarnation of the Son of God does not mean that Jesus Christ is part God and part man, nor does it imply that he is the result of a confused mixture of the divine and the human. He became truly man while remaining truly God. Jesus Christ is true God and true man. During the first centuries, the Church had to defend and clarify this truth of faith against the heresies that falsified it.

469 The Church thus confesses that Jesus is inseparably true God and true man. He is truly the Son of God who, without ceasing to be God and Lord, became a man and our brother:

"What he was, he remained and what he was not, he assumed," sings the Roman Liturgy. And the liturgy of St. John Chrysostom proclaims and sings: "O only-begotten Son and Word of God, immortal being, you who deigned for our salvation to become incarnate of the holy Mother of God and ever–virgin Mary, you who without change became man and were crucified, O Christ our God, you who by your death have crushed death, you who are one of the Holy Trinity, glorified with the Father and the Holy Spirit, save us!"

479 At the time appointed by God, the only Son of the Father, the eternal Word, that is, the Word and substantial Image of the Father, became incarnate; without losing his divine nature he has assumed human nature.

480 Jesus Christ is true God and true man, in the unity
of his divine person; for this reason he is the one and
only mediator between God and men.

481 Jesus Christ possesses two natures, one divine and
the other human, not confused, but united in the one
person of God's Son.

482 Christ, being true God and true man, has a human
intellect and will, perfectly attuned and subject to his
divine intellect and divine will, which he has in common
with the Father and the Holy Spirit.

483 The Incarnation is therefore the mystery of the
wonderful union of the divine and human natures in
the one person of the Word.

MARY

The role of Mary is also implied in the Jesus Prayer tradition.
In the fourteenth century an Athonite monastic hermit,
Maximus of Kapokalyvia, says to pray the Jesus Prayer "In
remembrance of Jesus and the Mother of God." This is unique
in the Jesus Prayer tradition, but it is derived from a logical
understanding of the incarnation. By the third century Mary
was being called the Theotokos or "bearer and mother of
God." At the Council of Ephesus in 431 this was authorita-
tively declared true. This is not meant to imply that she is
somehow a mother of God in heaven but that Jesus is fully

divine. He is Son of God and Son of Man. He is Son of God and Son of Mary. Most non-Catholics (and even some well-meaning Catholics!) misunderstand that all Mariology revolves around and exists only to explain and protect good Christology. Mary always points to Jesus.

THE CROSS AND RESURRECTION

The point of the incarnation was not merely for God to take on flesh and become human. The ultimate point of the incarnation is the cross and resurrection, the paschal mystery of Jesus Christ, which leads to the ascension and glory.

The Nicene Creed continues:

> For our sake he was crucified under Pontius Pilate,
> *he suffered death* and was buried,
> *and rose again on the third day*
> in *accordance with* the Scriptures.

The Eucharistic Prayer says that he takes on our humanity so that we might share in his divinity. This is paradox enough. But the cross and resurrection catapult us through the proverbial goalposts of the paradox of paradoxes!

Of the paradoxes of God, the Trinity and the incarnation St. Bonaventure says, "He is the divine sphere, the center of which is everywhere, and the circumference nowhere!" He says in *The Journey of the Mind [Soul] to God:*

> Because it is eternal and most present, it therefore encompasses and enters all duration as if it were at one and

the same time its center and circumference. Because it is utterly simple and the greatest, it is, therefore, totally within all things and totally outside them and thus "is an intelligible sphere whose center is everywhere and whose circumference is nowhere." . . . [He is] therefore, within all things, but not enclosed; outside all things, but not excluded; above all things, but not aloof; below all things, but not debased. Finally, because it is supremely one and all-inclusive, it is, therefore all in all.

A paradox is a seeming contradiction that proclaims a greater truth. Such paradoxes speed us from the objective doctrine *about* God concerning faith and morality, and take us directly into an intuitive experience *of* God. Such paradoxes include finding communion in solitude, hearing the word in silence, finding wealth in poverty and activity in sacred stillness. The greatest paradox is finding life through death. These paradoxes are found in the mystical traditions of all great faiths.

Christianity is unique in believing that Jesus Christ is the Paradox of paradoxes. He not only taught the way of finding life in death but became this Paradox of paradoxes through his death on a cross and in his resurrection and empty tomb. He not only points to the way, the truth and the life, but Jesus *is* the way, the truth and the life! After giving us monumental teachings about spirituality and God, all other great teachers died very early. The Buddha died from eating bad food. Krishna died in a petty clan war. Lau Tzu and Confucius both died thinking themselves abject failures. Moses and the prophets, except Elijah and Enoch, who were assumed into heaven, all died. Though they were great teachers, they all died. Only Jesus died and rose again! No other teacher or religious founder did so. In this he is utterly unique.

The Buddha said that he was only a finger pointing to the moon. His followers were not to look at him but to the moon. In his humanity Jesus was similar, for he can do nothing without the Father (Jn 5:19, 30). But in his divinity he is not so much the moon, which is used to describe Mary and the church, but the sun that illuminates the moon! Again, Buddhists will rightly say that we must not just teach the dharma, or law, but be the dharma. Well, Jesus did this more so than any other human being in history! Not only did he teach the paradox of dying and rising, he actually died and rose! No other teacher or mystic has done so in such a complete and stunning way.

St. Paul proclaims the wisdom of this paradoxical foolishness when he writes,

> For the message of the cross is foolishness to those who are perishing, but to us who are being saved it is the power of God. . . . Where is the wise? Where is the scribe? Where is the disputer of this age? Has not God made foolish the wisdom of this world? . . . It pleased God through the foolishness of the message preached to save

those who believe. For Jews request a sign, and Greeks seek after wisdom; but we preach Christ crucified, to the Jews a stumbling block and to the Greeks foolishness, but to those who are called, both Jews and Greeks, Christ the power of God and the wisdom of God. Because the foolishness of God is wiser than men, and the weakness of God is stronger than men. (1 Cor 1:18-25)

THE RESURRECTION

The resurrection of Jesus is also part of his incarnation and reveals God's plan for humanity. The Nicene Creed says:

On the third day he rose again
in fulfillment of the Scriptures;
he ascended into heaven
and is seated at the right hand of the Father.
He will come again in glory
to judge the living and the dead,
and his kingdom will have no end.

Through sin, we have all settled for a version of our humanity that is less than fully human. The incarnation reveals what true humanity is through the gift of divinity in Christ. The resurrection of Jesus shows us what the resurrection of the body will be for all of us! It was physical, yet beyond what we experience today. Thomas was invited to put his finger in to the wounds of the resurrected Jesus (Jn 20:25-29). And the resurrected Lord invited the disciples to eat fish with him by the Sea of Galilee (Jn 21:9-14). We too will have a body in the resurrection (Rom 8:11). The Apostle's Creed says:

I believe in the Holy Spirit,
the holy catholic Church,
the communion of saints,
the forgiveness of sins,
the resurrection of the body,
and the life everlasting. Amen.

But the resurrection body will be radically changed (1 Cor 15:50-55). Likewise, the New Jerusalem will come from heaven with streets of gold, "like transparent glass!" (Rev 21:21). This is so wonderful that we really cannot fully imagine it. Eye has not seen, ear has not heard, nor has it even dawned on the mind what awaits those who love him (1 Cor 2:9). Can I get a "Praise Jesus!" from anyone with an aging, injured or ill body on this one?

THE ASCENSION

The ascension of Jesus to heaven ushers in the giving of the Holy Spirit that we will briefly discuss in chapter six. He does not "leave us" but actually allows more intimate communion with him through the Spirit (Jn 14). It is also a promise of the ultimate goal of our resurrection! We will not be stranded here on this fallen earth but will enter fully into the realm of eternity and infinity for all eternity. This is good news!

In Eastern and Catholic Christianity the Assumption of Mary into Heaven further confirms this. While not formally proclaimed as a doctrine in the Catholic Church until 1950 by Pope Pius XII, it was widely believed in the early church and is accepted today by Roman Catholic, Orthodox and some Anglican Christians. The Eastern Church calls it the Dormition of Mary. The East believes that she died in order to fully experience communion with her Son. The West believes that more like Enoch or Elijah, and being without original (West) or ancestral (East) sin, she only appeared to die under the form of sleep. (Jesus died, though without sin, in order to carry our death.) It is even being accepted by some evangelicals and other non-Catholics.

As the Catechism of the Catholic Church says: "The Assumption of the Blessed Virgin is a singular participation in her Son's Resurrection and an anticipation of the resurrection of other Christians." As the Byzantine Liturgy, Troparion, Feast of the Dormition, August 15th says, "In giving birth you kept your virginity; in your Dormition you did not leave the world, O Mother of God, but were joined to the source of Life."

Jesus is the Redeemer. Mary is part of the redeemed and is the one who most perfectly cooperates with redemption through her Son, Jesus. Her assumption further confirms our assumption in the power of the ascension of Jesus Christ. (As noted earlier, it was already experienced by Enoch and Elijah [2 Kings 2:11; Heb 11:5].)

The fathers of the church often interpreted Revelation 12 to apply to Mary and her assumption as well. St. John of Damascus represents the tradition of the church of Jerusalem when he said:

> St. Juvenal, Bishop of Jerusalem, at the Council of Chalcedon (451), made known to the Emperor Marcian and Pulcheria, who wished to possess the body of the Mother of God, that Mary died in the presence of all the Apostles, but that her tomb, when opened, upon the request of St. Thomas, was found empty; wherefrom the Apostles concluded that the body was taken up to heaven.

This is the ultimate destination of our bodies as well! We have much to look forward to, and this is implied in the simple word *Jesus*!

PRACTICE

As we breathe in we allow ourselves to be transformed with the incarnation of Jesus, who took on our humanity so that we might share in his divinity. We allow ourselves to become fully human again through the divine gift of Jesus in our lives. We see ourselves in Mary, who believed the impossible so that Jesus could be born into this world. We become his mother, his brothers and sisters with each breath we take. We also dare to believe that love can conquer hatred, forgiveness can conquer judgment, justice can conquer vengeance, meekness can conquer pride, gentleness can conquer cruelty, Mary can conquer Eve, and Jesus can conquer Adam. All of this is in you and me, and it is conquered in every breath we breathe!

$$\underline{6}$$

Son of God, Part 3

Lord, Jesus Christ, *Son of God* . . .

THE CHURCH

The incarnation does not end with the body of Jesus. It also includes the church! The church is not some afterthought for those who follow Jesus. No, it is the continued presence of Jesus on earth even after he ascended back to the Father in heaven. St. Paul calls the church the "body of Christ" (1 Cor 12:27). As my song based on the words of St. Teresa of Ávila says, "Christ has no body now but yours."

When we pray the Jesus Prayer we must ask not only if we

are in full communion with Jesus but also in communion, common union, with the church. The Greek word for church is *ekklēsia*, which means "gathering." It was commonly used for Jewish synagogues, which were themselves the gathering of twelve or more male adults. Originally, for the proper practice of the Jesus Prayer it was essential to be part of the Orthodox or Catholic Church. Though this is still helpful today, it's not mandatory from an ecumenical perspective.

The Nicene Creed says,

I believe in one, holy,
catholic and apostolic Church.
I confess one baptism
for the forgiveness of sins
and I look forward to the resurrection of the dead
and the life of the world to come. Amen.

The church is "one," like a body that is unified in structural body, devotion of heart and doctrine of mind. Today the post-Schism, post-Reformation church is fractured into thousands of pieces, which was never the intent of those in the Schism or of reformers. Jesus says that the world will believe partly due to our unity. We are not united, and it scandalizes the world, which remains much in unbelief. Our hearts are increasingly united. Our theologians are also getting closer through genuine dialogue instead of argument and debate. But our structures are largely like dislocated, but not broken, bones in the body of Christ. We have much work to do!

The church is "holy." Despite our many failings and sins in membership and leadership, Jesus continues to keep us from major error and forgive us repeatedly, so that the gates of hell shall not prevail against us. We also have a huge witness of radical followers of Jesus in the succession of the saints that is the glory of our fellowship.

The church is "catholic." We are universal and full, and in communion with an apostolic faith that stretches unbroken from the time of Christ. In apostolic times this "communion," or "common union," was both invisible and visible. It still is today.

The church is "apostolic." Jesus, as the Word incarnate, gathered apostles who brought a living Word in the Spirit, and established living and Spirit-empowered churches and successors in leadership. From this apostolic tradition the Scriptures themselves were written and compiled, and form a complementary current in the wonderful river of the revelation of God in Christ and the church. Our entire life, worship and ministry are part of this ongoing stream of apostolic tradition that came directly from Jesus Christ.

Of course the church has leaders. Every tribe needs a council, and every council needs a chief. This is self-evident in human society. Jesus recognized this. Though Jesus had many disciples, including the Seventy (Lk 10), he chose twelve leaders as apostles from his disciples (Lk 6:12-16) and appointed one of the apostles to be the chief of the "tribal council" after he ascended. That apostle was Peter (Mt 16:18). Before the Scriptures were even complied by the church, successors to the apostles were established in every local church (Acts 14:23; Tit 1:5-9). As early as the first-century apostolic fathers Clement of Rome and Ignatius of Antioch, the church recognized the bishop of Rome as the leader of all the bishops who succeeded the apostles. Rome was preeminent because it was the final church of Peter and the place of the martyrdom of both Peter and Paul.

But the church is also personal and individual. The Holy Spirit was not only given to the leaders of the church (Jn 20:22) but was also poured forth on each Christian (Acts 2:3) and all who called on Jesus as Lord (1 Cor 12:3). Because we are one body by the Spirit, St. Paul spends significant energy explaining that when we are divided from one another, we are dividing ourselves from the body of Christ (1 Cor 12:12-21).

When we pray the Jesus Prayer, we must examine whether we are in communion with the entire church. Anything that is keeping us from full communion must be breathed out and completely let go. The way back to full communion is letting go of our old self through the dying of Jesus so that we can be raised up an entirely new person in Christ. We must let go of our attachments to our own ideas and agendas, even about the church and God.

For myself the key to this process is realizing that I am not God! Simple as this sounds, it is a real showstopper. Often I use God language to make myself God in my own eyes and in the church or monastic community. But I must admit that others might be smarter or wiser than me after all! Popes, bishops, presbyters, deacons and lay leaders usually get a lot of input and education before making decisions that affect the entire local or universal church. They love Jesus and pray just like I do, and even more so. Likewise with rank and file lay members. They are good people with gifts and talents from God. The Holy Spirit is poured out on them just like me. If I do not take the time to quietly, carefully and respectfully listen to them, I run the risk of cutting myself off from the full anointing of the Spirit of God.

THE EUCHARIST

The reality of the incarnation is extended to us sacramentally through the Eucharist, or what Latin Rite Catholics call "The Mass," many Protestants call "The Lord's Supper" and others call "Communion." To some extent these terms can be interchangeable, but they actually mean different specific things to each ecclesial gathering, so I will use the more universal and ancient word *Eucharist* throughout this book. I will also use the more ancient apostolic understanding of it. The Eucharist is a memorial sacrifice. It is both a symbol of Christ and his sacrifice, and a sacramental celebration that brings that reality into the present. It both symbolizes and affects the reality it celebrates.

The early church universally believed that Jesus was fully present sacramentally in the Eucharist. It was the central sacramental focus of their gatherings. In a way beyond mere human words, the Eucharist proclaims the incarnation as a reality that is living, not only two thousand years ago in Jesus, but right now, today in the church.

Early Christians also believed the Eucharist was a sacramental sacrifice. The presbyters were also called priests who led a priestly people. They still do so today. This is both a sacrifice of praise, and the sacramental memorial sacrifice of Jesus for us. This does not mean that the shedding of Jesus' blood is repeated in the Eucharist. That would nullify Scripture (Heb 7:27). It does mean that the sacrifice of Calvary is extended and sacramentally repeated in the Eucharist. It is what the Fathers called an "unbloody" sacrifice. It is in remembrance, but it is also very real. These are not just theological concepts or words!

This is very real, and intensely personal when rightly understood. Far too often we relegate the incarnation and the sacrifice of Calvary to something from two millennia ago in a largely foreign Middle Eastern culture. At best we see the sacrifice of Calvary in merely legal and positional ways. Many modern Western Christians believe in God, and only put that more essential belief in the wrapping of Christianity. Some accept the doctrines of Jesus without really having a personal love experience with Jesus. Sometimes the reality of the incarnation as an actual real presence and the sacrifice of Jesus as intensely personal eludes us, despite our doctrinal acceptance of the Christian faith. It remains in our heads, but does not drop to our hearts.

Rightly understood and experienced, the Eucharist brings

that sacrifice right into the present moment in a most powerful way. Jesus dies for me, now! Personally, when I rightly understand and pray the Eucharist, it reduces me to tears in response to the amazing love of Jesus for me personally.

The real presence and sacramental sacrifice of Jesus in the Eucharist brings the reality of the incarnation in a way more powerful than human words and theology. It is more than a mere religious rite. It is a sacred mystery, a sacrament that both fulfills and surpasses human understanding. And it is intensely personal and powerful when rightly understood.

This all magnifies the understanding of Jesus as Savior, and places that understanding in the context of the people he gathered, the leadership he established and the church he founded. Our salvation does not exist in a vacuum, but is a living personal love relationship with Jesus rooted in the context of a living people birthed from the living incarnation of the Word in Jesus Christ. It is personal, and intimate, and yet fully and righteously communal.

If we can see the presence of the Son of God in the church, we can also see him in the sacred mysteries, or sacraments, of the church. This is especially true in the Eucharist. The Eucharist is called the body of Christ in a most special sense. Jesus calls the elements of the Eucharist his flesh and blood (Jn 6:53-59). He also calls himself the bread of life in John 6:30-40, which is also his flesh for the life of the world. This is an allusion to the miraculous feeding—through manna— of the Jewish people during their exodus from Egypt. The

Eucharist is a similar miracle. The Eucharist is also a prefig-
uring of the marriage supper of the Lamb in Revelation 19:9.
The Eucharist is the new Passover for the followers of Jesus,
the sacramental presence of the Lamb of God. Jesus' statement
regarding his flesh and blood scandalized many followers,
which reveals that the people did not take his statement as a
mere symbol. As a result, many turned away from Jesus "and
walked with Him no more" (Jn 6:60-70).

The early church universally recognized that Jesus was
truly preset in the Eucharist. The only ones who held back
from the Eucharist were those who did not believe in the
fullness of the incarnation—the sacrifice of love of the Logos
in Jesus. All others participated joyfully in the mystery of
mysteries that uniquely brought Jesus into their midst. In his
Letter to Smyrnaeans St. Ignatius of Antioch said, "They [i.e.,
the Docetists] abstain from the Eucharist and from prayer,
because they do not confess that the Eucharist is the Flesh of
our Savior Jesus Christ, flesh which suffered for our sins and
which the Father, in his goodness, raised up again."

Today the Eucharist remains the "source and summit" of
our faith in Christ as Catholic Christians. Though great
music and preaching have been hallmarks of Catholic Christianity, in modern times they have fallen to a substandard
level. But this does not determine the spirituality of the
church. At the time of the Eucharist it no longer matters if the
music was good, the preaching was motivational or the
people were friendly. All that matters is that Jesus shows up.

And he does at every Mass! Because he always does, I figure I should too!

As I have gotten older, and hopefully a bit wiser, in my Catholic Christian faith I have found the Eucharist to be the most powerful common prayer experience in my life with other followers of Jesus. At every Eucharist I witness the continued incarnation of the Creator in creation. I experience the Logos in a way that is beyond expression through human words. I experience the Real Presence of the face of God in sacramental form in this earth. I experience the simple being of the dying and rising of Christ.

CONCLUSION

The three simple words *Son of God* imply almost our entire doctrinal, ecclesial and mystical aspects of our Christian faith. When we pray the Jesus Prayer we intuit these realities by simply breathing them in as an experience beyond human words or understanding. It really cannot be explained. It must be experienced to be appreciated.

Let's take a moment to pause by simply breathing in this reality of realities, this mystery of mysteries, this Savior of saviors, teacher of teachers and mystic of mystics. Breathe in the One who is God from God, Light from Light, true God from true God. Breathe in the incarnation, the dying and rising of Jesus, the church and the Eucharist. It is all there in one simple breath. Once you realize this you will never breathe the same again, and you will never be more than a simple breath from these awesome mysteries only found fully in Christ.

PRACTICE

We breathe in the reality of the church with this breath. Sometimes it is easy to breathe in Jesus or the Trinity or our personal salvation when it is not fleshed out in our lives with others. This breath allows Jesus to transform our lives with others in the gathering or church of Jesus Christ. We learn to listen in obedience before speaking, in responding rather than reacting, in sharing rather than arguing, in seeking to understand others rather than always demanding that others understand us. This brings us peace and communion to a fractured church. And it is not a mere ecclesiology, doctrine or structure. It happens as a mystical experience with every breath. With every breath we allow the teaching of the church in faith and morality to become a sacred mystery, a sacrament, that includes the elements and words of creation in a heavenly reality beyond words. Only then will the other things unfold in a real relationship with Jesus. Only then will the dislocated joints in the body of Christ be healed in Christ.

7

Have Mercy

Lord, Jesus Christ, Son of God,
have mercy . . .

$\mathcal{W}$e now move from the in breath of the Jesus Prayer to the out breath. We move from filling up to letting go. Breathing in fills and holds, but breathing out empties and lets go. It is appropriate that we begin the out breath with "have mercy." Here we begin to let go of all in our lives standing between us and the universal fullness or catholicity of all that comes before.

The word *mercy* has both Hebrew and Greek roots. There are several Hebrew words used for it. In a well-known Old Testament Scripture God says, "For I, the LORD your God, *am* a jealous God, visiting the iniquity of the fathers upon the children to the third and fourth *generations* of those who hate Me, but showing mercy to thousands, to those who love Me and keep My commandments" (Ex 20:5-6). The Hebrew word used here for mercy is *ḥesed*, which means "kindness, piety toward." It is variously translated into English as mercy, kindness, lovingkindness, goodness, kindly, merciful, favor, good, goodliness, pity.

In ancient Jewish ritual worship, the "mercy seat" was most important. It is mentioned in Exodus 25:17-22. The word there is *kappōret*, which refers to the lid that covered the Ark of the Covenant. God's presence was manifested above it (Ex 25:17-22). Only at specific times could the high priest come before the mercy seat (Lev 16:2). On the Day of Atonement the high priest made atonement for himself, the tabernacle and the people by a sin offering, which included sprinkling blood on this lid (Lev 16:13-15).

The last Hebrew word we will look at is found in Psalm 51, the great psalm of heartfelt and contrite repentance to God. The word is *ḥānan*, which means "to bend or stoop in kindness to an inferior; to favor, bestow." It can also mean gracious, merciful, supplication, favor, pity and fair.

The Greek words are similar. They are *eleeō* or *eleos*. Both are used in the scriptural sources for the Jesus Prayer. They are also related to the familiar Kyrie Eleison, "Lord, have mercy," we recite toward the beginning of every Mass. (We have already examined the Greek origins of *Lord*, *kyrios*, which give us Kyrie.) The Greek *hilastērion* is also used for "merciful" and refers to the one that will bear the full weight of punishment for the sins of another. The tax collector cries out for this mercy in the parable of the Pharisee and tax collector in Luke 18:9-14. Through his crucifixion and resurrection, Jesus became and *is* this atoning mercy (1 Jn 2:2).

Essentially, mercy means "compassion." But a significant detail is often overlooked. Mercy is compassion plus empathy. Compassion already moves toward empathy in itself. The biblical word for compassion is *splanchnizomai*, which means "to feel mercy from the very bowels of your being." It comes from the word *splanchnon*, which means "tender," but also "bowels and intestines." It comes from the gut and is not merely peripheral. It is a tender mercy that comes from your deepest being in a way that enlivens the emotions without being immobilized. It is gutsy!

But empathy is even more. *The Complete Word Study Dictionary* says, "Eleos specifically means a feeling of empathy, fellow feeling with misery, compassion." This inclusion of empathy is most significant. Empathy is more than sympathy. Sympathy is from the outside in. It is good, and is encouraged by St. Paul who says, "Finally, all of you, be of one mind, sympathetic, loving toward one another, compassionate, humble" (1 Pet 3:8 RNAB). The Greek for sympathy is *sympathēs*, and means to literally walk with someone else in their suffering. Walking alongside of someone is a high standard and hard to meet. But empathy goes even deeper. It "walks a mile in my shoes," not merely feeling sympathy as I walk the mile. It is walking with someone, not from the outside in, but from the inside out.

When we ask for mercy from God we are asking him to be inside of us. This gives special significance to the incarnation, where the Word became flesh and dwelled among us, and with Pentecost, where Jesus takes up residence inside of us via his Holy Spirit. But it was also true all along because of his omnipresence. What changes is our relationship with his presence. He is merciful from within us, more internal to us than we are to ourselves. He reveals a mercy that is the very best of the best for us.

St. Augustine essentially says that God loves us more than we love ourselves, knows us better than we know ourselves, and is closer to us than we are to ourselves. St. Paul says that no one knows a person but the spirit of the person: "For what man knows the things of a man except the spirit of the man which is in him? Even so no one knows the things of God except the Spirit of God" (1 Cor 2:11). But God's Spirit knows us better than we know ourselves. He is also closer to us than we are to ourselves. Therefore, since he is love, he loves us more than we love ourselves. That is quite a reality!

In his *Confessions* St. Augustine says,

> No one knows what he himself is made of, except his own spirit within him, yet there is still some part of him which remains hidden even from his own spirit; but

you, Lord, know everything about a human being because you have made him. . . . Let me, then, confess
what I know about myself, and confess too what I do
not know, because what I know of myself I know only
because you shed light on me, and what I do not know
I shall remain ignorant about until my darkness becomes like bright noon before your face.

Augustine also says, "While following the flesh, it is You
whom I sought, but You Yourself were closer to me than my
inmost self and higher than the high-point of myself."

Sin has separated us from ourselves and given us an incomplete understanding of our own person. We have settled
for only two of our faculties—the body and soul—and allowed ourselves to forget the spirit. Only Jesus can restore us
to the person God made us to be, to the person who exists
deep within us but has been covered up all our life. That
original person of the spirit is like a child that went to sleep.
Jesus awakens that child, and by allowing the old, false so-
phisticated self to die with Christ, that original child of the
spirit is "born again" in a full love relationship with the Spirit
of God in Christ.

Don't we often feel disconnected with ourselves? We walk
around in our flesh, but are not in touch with our spirit and
soul. Therefore, we travel everywhere but do not seem fully
present anywhere. This is because we have settled for a self-
identity that limits us to senses, emotions and thoughts alone.

We rarely break through to the intuitions of the deepest spirit in his Spirit.

As we have seen elsewhere in this book, St. Paul says that we are spirit, soul and body (1 Thess 5:23). Our spirit is the faculty of intuition that builds on the faculties of the body and soul, but surpasses them. The spirit has the faculty to intuit eternity in an instant and infinity in a finite moment. It is this faculty that St. Paul says is first, not last, on the list. But we usually operate with the senses and thoughts alone, and then find our emotions in turmoil. We become enslaved to ego-attached senses and thoughts, and become prisoners of unruly emotions. Then, no matter how much we indulge ourselves we wonder why we are not happy!

We beg God for mercy in the Jesus Prayer. We beg God to be with us, inside of us. We beg God, who knows who we truly are, to reveal our true selves to ourselves. We beg the one who is closer to us than we are to ourselves to bring us back into union with ourselves through communion with all in Christ. How do we get there?

In a sense Jesus has already gotten us there by taking on our humanity so that we might share in his divinity. He gets right inside our humanity so that we might rediscover our created divinity. But this is not just a corporate matter. It is deeply personal and intimate. We get there through personally embracing the cross and resurrection of Jesus. We die to the old disordered and incomplete self. Then the real self can be resurrected in Christ.

PRACTICE

So, let's take a moment to pray the Jesus Prayer. Breathe in the universal catholicity and fullness of the Christian faith. Lord . . . Jesus . . . Christ . . . Son of God.

Now let's breathe out and let go. *Have mercy.* Ah! As you let go of the old, incomplete self, can you feel all the tensions and stresses dissipate? That letting go calms emotions, settles thoughts and even heals the body. Just rest a bit before we turn the page. There is still more.

8

On Me

Lord, Jesus Christ, Son of God,
have mercy *on me* . . .

Catholics are very big on community. Popes John Paul II and Benedict XVI have described Catholic spirituality as "communion" (Latin, *communio*). In Scripture the Greek word *koinōnia* is used, which means "fellowship," "community" or "communion." It has both ecclesial and eucharistic overtones. It is used of the first Christian community in Jerusalem, which became the model of all religious life in the church: "And they continued steadfastly in the apostles' doctrine and fellowship [common life], in the breaking of bread, and in prayers" (Acts 2:42). *Koinōnia* also refers to sharing in something, "through the proof of this ministry, they glorify God for the obedience of your confession to the gospel of Christ, and for *your* liberal sharing with them and all men" (2 Cor 9:13), and making a contribution, "It pleased those from Macedonia and Achaia to make a certain contribution for the poor among the saints who are in Jerusalem" (Rom 15:26). It also has rather obvious eucharistic and church connotations: "The cup of blessing which we bless, is it not the communion of the blood of Christ? The bread which we break, is it not the communion of the body of Christ? For we, *though* many, are one bread *and* one body; for we all partake of that one bread" (1 Cor 10:16-17).

When I became a Catholic in 1978, it was this communal emphasis of the church that drew me. I had come from a Lone Ranger spirituality in the Jesus Movement. While there were many intentional, and sometimes down right cultish and just weird, communal expressions of the movement, it remained so firmly fixed in an emphasis on the personal that it lapsed into the individualism that is so endemic in American culture. In other words, in its attempt to transform American culture it was perverted by the culture it was trying to save. Instead of being in the world and not of it, it became worldly! I sought a communal expression that was ancient and time tested, that avoided the extreme I saw in the Jesus Movement and the evangelical world. I found it especially in the more intentional Franciscan expressions of Catholicism, and even in the local Catholic parish.

But sometimes we Catholics go too far with the communal emphasis. At my parish missions I jokingly say that when I ask married men if they are good Catholics, many say, "Sure, my wife goes to Mass every Sunday!" It always gets a hearty laugh. We sometimes take our communal emphasis so far that we forget the need for a personal encounter with Christ. This is one of the gifts of the Jesus Prayer. It brings us back to the personal.

In the Prayer we say "on me." Salvation is personal. It is intimate. No one can do it for us. St. Paul says that we should "bear one another's burdens, and so fulfill the law of Christ" (Gal 6:2). But just a few verses later he says, "But let each one examine his own work, and then he will have rejoicing in himself alone, and not in another. For each one shall bear his own load" (Gal 6:4-5). While the Greek text uses two different words, *baros* and *phortion*, they both can mean "burden, load or weight."

Remember the Athonite monk who asked, "What do you think brother, are we being saved today?" As he asked the question he wept. Remember our reflection on receiving the Eucharist? The Eastern tradition says that we should not let anyone convince us that we cannot weep every time we receive Communion. Wow! I do not see many tears at most celebrations of the Eucharist. (Admittedly, I always see a few.) How can I not weep when I reflect on what Jesus did, and does, for me personally?

When Jesus was born, died and rose, it was personal. It

was intimate. When he was cradled in Mother Mary's arms, and taught by St. Joseph, it was personal. When he went into solitary temptation in the desert, it was personal. When John the Baptist baptized him in the Jordan River, it was personal. When he reached to touch the sick, it was personal. When he wept at the death of Lazarus, it was personal. When sent the Holy Spirit, it was personal. And especially when he died naked upon the cross, it was personal. How can I not respond personally to such a personal gift of love?

I remember a brother in our community who took a walk through the hills and woods around Little Portion Monastery in Arkansas. He came back weeping. I asked him if he was okay. He responded by saying that while walking it dawned upon him that Jesus would have come into this world, died on a cross, risen and ascended, and given the Holy Spirit to the entire church even if he was the only person to ever receive him. Whoa! He realized that Jesus died for him personally. His response was deeply personal, and even intimate. There are parts of it that he could describe, but other parts were so deep and intimate that they could only be expressed with tears.

This personal response to Jesus is symbolized in the sacraments, especially those celebrated more communally. We often receive the Eucharist in a line with lots of other folks. It is communal. But it is also personal. At the time of receiving Jesus in the Eucharist we must make a personal decision to stand up, step out in faith, and come forward to receive. Only

those with special needs do not do so, and we bring the Eucharist to them in their seats. But for most of us a decision
must be made. (Some people choose to sit in their pew and
privately pray—we have all abstained from time to time.)
Participation is encouraged communally, but it is not de-
manded. Each individual must choose to respond or not. We
can stand up and go forward or remain seated. It is a personal
decision to receive Jesus.

Some people say that Catholics do not do altar calls. But it
is untrue. Every Mass is an altar call! Every Mass requires a
personal decision for Christ. And we do it, but not out of law
alone (though it is not a bad law that says to attend church
every Sunday and on holy days), but out of love. It is love
answering love, as Scripture says, "We love Him because He
first loved us" (1 Jn 4:19). It is a love response to the ultimate
love gift of God for us personally in Jesus. He lays down his
life out of love so that we might live in love again. How can
we not respond?

Even in the Psalms we see such a personal response to the
love and forgiveness of God. The following excerpts from
Psalm 51, the *Miserere*, cannot be prayed without an intense
personal love and conversion:

> Have mercy on me, God, in accord with your
>   merciful love;
>   in your abundant compassion blot out my
>   transgressions.

Thoroughly wash away my guilt;
    and from my sin cleanse me.
For I know my transgressions;
    my sin is always before me. . . .

Cleanse me with hyssop, that I may be pure;
    wash me, and I will be whiter than snow.
You will let me hear gladness and joy;
    the bones you have crushed will rejoice.

Turn away your face from my sins;
    blot out all my iniquities.
A clean heart create for me, God;
    renew within me a steadfast spirit.
Do not drive me from before your face,
    nor take from me your holy spirit.
Restore to me the gladness of your salvation;
uphold me with a willing spirit. . . .

Lord, you will open my lips;
    and my mouth will proclaim your praise.
My sacrifice, O God, is a contrite spirit;
    a contrite, humbled heart, O God, you will not
      scorn. (Ps 51:3-5, 9-14, 17-19 RNAB)

The Jesus Prayer brings us into intimate communion with these realities with every breath we take. We breathe in the wonders of God in Christ and the church, and breathe out anything standing between us and a full communion with these wonders of salvation in Jesus. It is personal and as intimate as the intimate breath of God, the gift of his Spirit.

If we reflect on this we will be reduced to tears. I know that I am. At every Mass and with every breath I can intuit these awesome realities beyond my ability to fully understand. Yet I know them with a knowing that is deeper than my mind or emotions. It is certainly deeper than my senses alone. It is something that must be intuited on the level of the spirit in his Spirit.

I am also reduced to tears when I pray the Jesus Prayer, especially in private. Solitude is a marvelous tool to help with this. It is like singing. Sometimes it is easier to sing first in the shower before we try to sing in public! Likewise with the Jesus Prayer: It is often best to start in a private place, in solitude, before we try to bring these gifts to the public. Being reduced and uplifted to that which is beyond words is personal and intimate. Only when we are comfortable with this experience privately can we begin to express it publically.

I find myself like the sinful woman at the Pharisee's dinner.

And behold, a woman in the city who was a sinner, when she knew that *Jesus* sat at the table in the Pharisee's house, brought an alabaster flask of fragrant oil, and stood at His feet behind *Him* weeping; and she began to wash his feet with her tears, and wiped them with the hair of her head; and she kissed His feet and anointed *them* with the fragrant oil. (Lk 7:37-38)

The Pharisee complains that this is a sinner and she is embarrassing everyone. Jesus says,

> Do you see this woman? I entered your house; you gave Me no water for My feet, but she has washed My feet with her tears and wiped *them* with the hair of her head. You gave Me no kiss, but this woman has not ceased to kiss My feet since the time I came in. You did not anoint My head with oil, but this woman has anointed My feet with fragrant oil. Therefore I say to you, her sins, which *are* many, are forgiven, for she loved much. But to whom little is forgiven, the *same* loves little. (Lk 7:44-47)

Tears flow from a heart of love. Her tears are personal and flow from a heart of intimate love.

PRACTICE

So to conclude, let's pray together:

Breathe in: "Lord, Jesus Christ, Son of God, have mercy *on me . . .*"

As we breathe in allow Jesus to bring his mercy to us from the inside out. Allow yourself to be aware that he is closer to us than we are to ourselves. Know that he understands us better than we understand ourselves. Now, allow yourself to enter into the forgiveness that only God can bring in Christ. This is not a mere theological doctrine or idea. It is a reality, and it is breath by breath. It sets us free from sin with every breath we breathe!

9

A Sinner

Lord, Jesus Christ, Son of God,
have mercy on me, *a sinner*.

$\mathcal{T}$he words *a sinner* conclude the Jesus Prayer. But they were not part of the original version. In fact, neither was "have mercy on me." The original Jesus Prayer ended with the positive "Son of God." The need for mercy and salvation that is personal is implicit. However, rather humorously, the fathers added these to keep the new members of the monastic community in their place! Calistas and Ignatius's work *Directions to Hesychasts* says, "As regards the words, 'Have mercy on me,' . . . it was added by the fathers chiefly for those who are still infants in the work of virtue, the beginners in the imperfect stage."

I am reminded of a brilliant Franciscan psychologist and scholar of Franciscan spirituality who was a rather typical left-leaning intellectual on some issues. Then he was made Novice Master! He shared with me that he rather quickly re-instituted that the novices would wear their habits in the house and while doing ministry. He also reinstated some other traditional Franciscan practices that had been lost. He felt that if they made sacrifices for secular jobs to make money, they should also learn to sacrifice personal prefer-ences for the sake of their vocation in Christ and the church.

He concluded by saying that he told the novices, "We will tell you what it is to be a Franciscan, you will not tell us!" Sometimes new members are a bit full of themselves; they tend to quickly judge older members who have learned to live their vocations for the long haul. Similarly, the inclusion of the last words of the Jesus Prayer were instituted by the fathers for the young monks to remind them that they were sinners and not yet experts in monastic life!

A foundational understanding of ourselves is that we are sinners. All religions teach that something has gone wrong, and life is incomplete at best. Otherwise, there would be no need of religion (or any teaching at all, for that matter)! The Judeo-Christian story includes the expulsion of Adam and Eve from the Garden of Eden. Taoists speak of a past Golden Age. Buddhists say that we live in the darkest era of all eras. The train might be moving, but it has a wheel or two off the track. It is rolling with a resistance that will drag the whole train down, which of course places in jeopardy the safety of its passengers. Christians call the problem sin.

Scripture says, "all have sinned and fall short of the glory of God" (Rom 3:23). The word for sin in this passage is *hamartia*, which means "to miss the mark" and to "wander" from the path of God's law and Word. Wandering from the path is also a familiar symbol for Eastern religions. One of the major Buddhist scriptures is the Dhammapada—the path of the teaching.

Missing the mark is a notion used in Greek archery tournaments. When the archers shot an arrow toward the target, they would usually hit the target but miss the bull's eye—the center. The spotter would shout *hamartia* (sin)! This has radical ramifications for the normal Christian conception of sin.

We are created in God's image to seek goodness, truth, beauty, love and justice. We shoot our arrows generally in the right direction. Very few of us turn 180-degrees from the target, from God. Even when we think we are not seeking God, we are seeking him nonetheless.

I once sat next to a satanist on a flight from Chicago to Los Angeles, the city of angels! I was dressed in my monastic habit, so we got into a conversation. Of course we politely disagreed about God! What struck me was that the poor guy could not get away from God even when opposing him. He genuinely thought that evil was good, that destroying was the *best* thing. So, he could not get away from trying to do the *best* even by doing the worst!

I have had similar conversations with atheists. What many of the more thoughtful atheists object to is the limiting of the spirituality of what we call God through organized religion and theology. (This is reflected in the book *The End of Faith* by Sam Harris.) Some atheists would say that they accept the idea of an ineffable spirituality and the "Other," but they reject limiting such an Other to a religious notion of God. They might say that they accept spirituality, but reject religion. I must admit that the caricature of much of our Western theology falls desperately short of the rich reality of God, even by traditional standards. We often stay tragically trapped in our heads. Indeed, genuine Christian mysticism, and the Jesus Prayer itself, leads us from the doctrinal head to the mystical heart, which ultimately leads to God through the way, truth and life of Jesus Christ. So, even though they call themselves atheists and nonbelievers, they are really serving the true God. I suspect that they are really agnostics (those who are open to God but have yet to encounter him) rather than atheists, though they would not think of themselves as such.

So, the reality of sin might seem less radical than we initially think. But that does not mean that it is not deadly! "The wages of sin *is* death" (Rom 6:23) and "When sin reaches maturity it gives birth to death" (Jas 1:15 RNAB). Sin might only amount to a wheel off the track of the train, but a derailed train kills!

TEMPTATION

How do we fall into sin? St. James gives us a hint:

> Blessed *is* the man who endures temptation; for when
> he has been approved, he will receive the crown of life
> which the Lord has promised to those who love Him.
> Let no one say when he is tempted, "I am tempted by
> God"; for God cannot be tempted by evil, nor does He
> Himself tempt anyone. But each one is tempted when
> he is drawn away by his own desires and enticed. Then,
> when desire has conceived, it gives birth to sin; and sin,
> when it is full-grown, brings forth death.
>
> Do not be deceived, my beloved brethren. (Jas 1:12-16)

St. Augustine describes three stages of temptation:
thought, entertainment and action. In other words, we first
think of sin, then we toy with it, and then we do it! According
to Augustine the first stage is universal and is not yet
sin. Even Jesus was "in all *points* tempted *as we are*, *yet*
without sin" (Heb 4:15). Being tempted is not a sin. But internally
playing with, entertaining and acting on that entertaining
is. This can destroy our attitudes and emotions. Then
sin begins the serious work of bringing death to relationships
and to the entire world.

The Eastern fathers use a bit more complex series of stages,
ranging from five to seven. Personally, and perhaps as a Westerner,
I find Augustine's description the easiest to understand
and the most helpful in daily life.

THE EIGHT THOUGHTS

The Eastern fathers excel in understanding the interior psychology and spiritual process of how thoughts that lead to vice actually work. These are called the *logizomai* in Scripture. The root is *logos* or "word," and is sometimes used with the preposition *dia*, forming the source of the word *dialogue*. This is how Jesus uses the word: "For out of the heart proceed evil thoughts [*dialogismos*], murders, adulteries, fornications, thefts, false witness, blasphemies" (Mt 15:19). This sets the stage for the teaching of the Eastern fathers.

The fathers teach that all vices proceed from eight thoughts. In the West we refer to these as "The Seven Capital (or Cardinal) Sins." The list of seven was complied by Pope Gregory the Great (c. 540–604) and brought into the East through St. John Climacus, the seventh-century abbot of St. Catherine's Monastery in the Sinai.

However, the "Eight Thoughts" came first from the monastic Christian East through Evagrius Ponticus (345–399), and John Cassian (c. 360–435), who brought monasticism from Egypt and Palestine to southern Gaul (present-day France). The Eight Thoughts are gluttony, sexual sin, avarice, anger, bitterness, boredom, self-glorification and pride. Evagrius puts bitterness before anger, and Cassian places anger before bitterness. Three of these—gluttony, avarice and self-glorification—lead to the other five, from which all vices flow.

There is a logic to the list. A small sensual sin (gluttony) leads to big sensual sin (sexual sin). Gluttony is eating or drinking when we do not need to. It is the proverbial comfort-food syndrome. Sexual sin is activity that violates mutual self-giving in the context of marriage and for the purpose of procreation. Avarice is the need to control possessions and relationships. When we do not get the sensual gratification or control we want, we first get frustrated and then angry. When anger is not healed, it hides in the inner recesses of the heart and soul as bitterness, which infects everything in our lives. When we get bitter, we get bored with the spiritual life and God, which used to motivate us. Thus we just go to sleep! The need for constant affirmation and self-glorification in little things leads to full-on pride if left unchecked.

The fathers also list some cures.

Gluttony is healed through moderate fasting. The monastic fast is disciplined eating of sufficient but reduced amounts of food and drink every day. The fathers do not recommend extreme fasting because this often gives way to gorging after the fast.

Sexual sin is overcome through vigils and manual labor. When we get tempted at night, we must get up, go to the church and pray. It is more difficult to sin while really praying. Likewise, if we do hard labor during the day, we will be too tired to fool around and get into sexual trouble.

Avarice is overcome through living in community under an abbot. The same could be said about well-ordered families or professions. Anyone who has lived in community, including family, knows that it is hard to maintain control when compromising daily with others for the greater good. This is found in big things, but is really tested and proven in the little things of life.

Anger is overcome through forgiveness. If we let the old self truly die, then there is no old self to get angry. Obsessing and fuming in silence is unhealthy, but letting go and letting God calms anger. St. Francis says that any sinner should be called back to forgiveness simply by looking into our eyes.

Bitterness and dejection are overcome through praise and thanks. We become people of praise with an attitude of gratitude. This is found when we realize that "all things work together for good to those who love God, to those who are called according to *His* purpose" (Rom 8:28). When we see things this way, we can even praise and thank God for our big and little troubles. It is hard to stay negative with such attitudes. Suddenly we see the glass as half full rather than half empty.

Boredom (sometimes called the noonday devil or *ascedia* because it strikes the monk in the heat of the day with an overwhelming desire to simply go to sleep) is not overcome through some esoteric technique. Boredom is overcome by good, old-fashioned work. When bored, do something for God and others! This was the advice that the angel of God gave to St. Antony of the Desert when he was struggling with boredom in prayer, and it worked!

Self-glorification is overcome by giving God glory. The desire for glory sits on the shoulders of everyone, especially public speakers and figures. It appeals to our ego when we do things well and wounds the ego when we do not. St. Francis said that we are to give constant glory to God whenever we do things well and are praised or thanked for it.

Pride is overcome by meditation on the passion of Jesus. This meditation involves the creative use of our imaginations to visualize the unfolding details of Jesus' dying and rising. These events are graphic and personal. They were done out of personal love for each of us. We simply cannot meditate on his suffering and glorification for each of us and persist in pride. Only those who do not fully meditate, or are hardhearted will not have their pride simply melted away.

These are the Eight Thoughts that tempt us to sin, or miss the mark, and stray from the path of God. The fathers say that they are interconnected, and they are also connected to their opposites, the interconnected virtues. They form a sort of ladder on which we either ascend to or descend from the throne of God. As St. Peter Damian says, we either go up or down in daily Christian life. If we try to stand still, we fall from the ladder and fail.

St. Hesychios says that the Jesus Prayer is most helpful in overcoming all these tempting thoughts: "Whenever we are filled with evil thoughts, we should throw the invocation of our Lord Jesus Christ into their midst. Then, as experience has taught us, we shall see them instantly dispersed like smoke into the air."

SPIRIT, SOUL, BODY

The interconnected relationship of virtues and vices is similar to that of the Pauline anthropology of spirit, soul and body. Sin has turned us upside down. We now place the priority of the body first. We then get attached to this incomplete self-identity and cling to sensual comfort, good feelings and personal ideas and agendas. When the senses, emotions or thoughts of our bodies and souls are threatened, we become unhappy and project and inflict our unhappiness onto everyone we meet. Though imperceptible at first, after a while it destroys the health and success of everything in our lives.

The way back to the primacy of the spirit in his Spirit is through dying to our old selves. The fruit of the spirit in his Spirit is love, joy, peace, patience, kindness, generosity, faithfulness, gentleness, self-control. Paul informs us how our lives are made fruitful: "Those who belong to Christ [Jesus] have crucified their flesh with its passions and desires. If we live in the Spirit, let us also follow the Spirit" (Gal 5:24-25 RNAB).

CONCLUSION

So sin is less serious than what we think because even

sinners seek goodness. But it is more serious than we think because it kills if left unchecked. Sin initially affects the little things of life, but it soon leads to big and most serious things.

This reminds of a commonly accepted apocryphal story of Martin Luther about sin during his table talk with young students. Though most Lutherans would not accept that this story is true, nor does it represent the current understanding of sin by most Protestants I know, it illustrates a good point about commonly misunderstood concepts of sin. The story says that Luther described sin as a power that turns the human soul to a dung heap. The sacrifice of Christ is like a layer of pure, white snow that covers that dung heap. When God the Father looks down from heaven he sees a pile of lily-white snow. But kick it, and it will send up the smell of a dung heap! The problem with the analogy is that it causes us to essentially think of the human being as a pile of dung. When we think this of ourselves, we project it onto others. This is a very negative and even dangerous image. It implies that Jesus' work of the atonement does not change the human soul for the better.

St. Bonaventure uses another analogy that is far more healthy and accurate. The human soul, he says, is like a mirror created to reflect the beautiful and wonderful image of God. Sin is like dust and dirt that first dulls the image. Then it partially obscures the image. Eventually obscures the image altogether. But there is good news: Jesus does windows!

When Jesus cleanses us from sin we can once more reflect the image of God.

This analogy has more positive implications. It means that even the worst sinner has the potential to reflect the beautiful image of God. It gives us a positive and hopeful image of others and ourselves.

So we are all sinners. We all miss the mark and stray from the path. Jesus comes to lovingly forgive and gently lead us back to the path for our journey to God through Christ. But we never walk the path perfectly during this life. Only Jesus is perfect. So, we need a constant reminder of the reality of sin, forgiveness and empowerment in righteousness. This is true even for those who have walked the way of Jesus for many years. None of us is beyond this most basic aspect of the gospel of Jesus Christ.

The ultimate cure for sin is Jesus. He bears our sins on the cross and rises up so that we might be lifted up from sin as well. He takes on our humanity so that we might share in his divinity; he becomes man to lead us back to God. He must be fully human and sinless in order to bear the sins of all others. He must be fully God in order to bear the sins of more than one other human being. Mary is kept from sin so that she might bear the Son of God (i.e., she is the Theotokos) who will die on the cross so that all might live. This is a mystery of mysteries that defies human logic, but it balances our logic in a refreshing, redeeming and unique way. Jesus really is the answer.

PRACTICE

We conclude by breathing out our sin, all of our sin! Let it go completely. Don't hang on to or to try to rationalize, justify or theologize it. Let it go. It will only wear you out! Breathe out and let go. As we do this we experience true healing. Our dirty mirror is washed clean in Christ, and we begin to reflect the beautiful image of God again. Breathe out and shine.

10

Conclusion

$\mathscr{A}$s we conclude these reflections, the first thing that I would encourage you going forward is to set aside a time and place to pray the Jesus Prayer daily. Hesychia, or sacred stillness, is necessary to initially engage in the Prayer and requires some uninterrupted time and space.

Regarding space, I recommend a prayer room or prayer corner in your house or monastic cell. You can also go to your local parish or monastic church, especially in the presence of some holy icons or the Blessed Sacrament. But this often requires traveling, which is, in itself, an interruption to contemplative peace. Ideally it should be in your dwelling.

For those with limited space, as in a small house or apartment, set aside part of a room otherwise used for normal daily activities. I remember visiting one of our domestic members (those of our integrated monastic community who live in their own homes or "domiciles") who had a swivel chair in his living room. During prayer he swiveled around to the prayer corner, and during daily social life he swiveled to the living room!

The space should be clean and uncluttered, with maybe only a few holy icons and a crucifix to focus the eye. You could also include a holy book like the Bible or a collection of the apostolic or monastic fathers. The Philokalia is the best for the practice of the Jesus Prayer, but it is not mandatory. Anything more will become a distraction.

POSTURE

The fathers also recommended a unique posture for the practice of the Prayer. They sat on low stools, pulled their legs up to their chests and gazed at their navels, for they considered that the gravitational center or heart of the body. (This is where we get the term *navel gazers!* In the West we say that such people are "so heavenly minded, that they are no earthly good!" It's the same thing. But we do not want to get so obsessed about the Prayer, or prayer in general, that we no longer function effectively with the love, truth and responsibility that Jesus reestablishes to our once wayward lives.)

Posture is important! We have found that the classical Jesus Prayer posture is simply impractical for most Westerners. By the time we are old enough to go deeper than our typically shallow American Christian expressions, we are often to too old and stiff for such calisthenics! So, we suggest sitting comfortably but attentively in a straight-back chair, with feet flat on the floor and hands resting comfortably but intentionally on the lap. The initial discomfort of attention to posture at the beginning will move past being distracted by the aches and pains from bad posture as you get into the Prayer.

TIME

For most contemporary Westerners, finding time for private prayer is tough. But it is vital. St. Francis of Assisi said that if we can give daily time to food and drink (and God knows we do that!), we can also give daily time for God! This is true regarding the Eucharist, but it is also true regarding private prayer and devotion.

Many suggest starting with five minutes a day for the Jesus Prayer. I suggest taking twenty minutes twice a day, once in the morning and once in the evening. We certainly give more than that to our meals. If you cannot do it twice, do it once! If only once, I recommend the morning. But many object and say that the house is too busy or they are too groggy in the morning. So, okay, try the evening. However, many object and say that they are too tired to do anything but watch TV. All right, I can see their point, though the excuses are really getting flimsy by now! In that case practice "supine meditation" on your bed! But do it! The problem with praying in bed is that we tend to fall asleep when meditating in bed, which is a good reason to additionally practice the Jesus Prayer in bed at night. But that is not the same as praying attentively throughout the day.

Out of twenty minutes we will probably only get two minutes of good contemplative prayer in the spirit in his Spirit. The rest will be settling into and coming out of the Prayer through the senses, thoughts and emotions of the body and soul. While praying we go from the body to the mind and on to the heart. And we must come back from the prayer of the heart to enliven the mind and body in the name of Jesus Christ. But two minutes of genuine contemplative prayer in the spirit through his Spirit will be enough to empower your entire day with all the love, joy and peace you will need to face any challenge in Christ.

COMMUNITY

I also suggest joining a group of like-minded folks who are also seeking this way of deeper prayer. Ideally this will include those seeking the way of the Jesus Prayer. But it might be a group of people seeking a deeper contemplative and monastic life in the midst of the world. Such groups are found attached to monasteries throughout the world. Ours are called domestics, those who live our way of life in their own homes. Historically in the West groups have been attached to the major spiritual families like the Benedictines and Franciscans. These are often called "oblates," "seculars" or "associates." While these are Catholic groups, they all welcome non-Catholics, and many of these groups include up to 50 percent non-Catholics. There are other non-Catholic monastics that have their own groupings as well.

Spiritual Fathers and Mothers

In the Christian East the role of the spiritual father and mother is seen as essential to the practice of the Jesus Prayer. In the West we call them spiritual directors, but they are different in character and tone. In the East we briefly, and without elaboration or excuses, reveal our thoughts to spiritual fathers and mothers almost daily. The use of the Eight Thoughts is very helpful to assist and expedite our spiritual inventory. They give rather classic responses with the incarnational touch of a living, breathing person walking with us. This face-to-face instruction makes a great difference.

In the East they say that it is really not enough to read books about spiritual life or the Jesus Prayer. You must also have a spiritual father or mother as a guide. But they also caution (as do the masters of the West) that a bad spiritual director is worse than no spiritual director. In that case reading the Bible and the apostolic and monastic fathers, especially in the Philokalia, is sufficient. But the best and safest way is through reading, practice and the guidance of a spiritual father or mother.

Church and Sacraments

The Jesus Prayer is never a replacement for active life in the church and reception of the sacraments or sacred mysteries. To the contrary, the Prayer makes all this come to new life in Christ! Suddenly, instead of having to go to church, we *want* to go to church! The church is the true spiritual home where those with apostolic authority authentically interpret the apostolic tradition and the Scriptures, which are the earliest written record of this authority. For the Orthodox and Catholics this is confirmed through apostolic succession in patriarchs and bishops, and the Petrine ministry in the bishop of Rome. The sacraments, especially the Eucharist, are the means through which the grace of God in Jesus Christ is both symbolized and affected, or caused, and confirmed. It is the simple and silent act that proclaims the Logos more profoundly than mere human words. It is the liturgical and sacramental act that encompasses all the contemplation and activity of Christ on earth. After praying the Jesus Prayer, all these wonderful realities take on a whole new power in the Spirit, for our spirit has been awakened, born again and enlivened in the Spirit of God through the dying and rising of Christ.

PRACTICE

Now we come back to where we began: the simple practice of the Jesus Prayer, "Lord Jesus Christ, Son of God, have mercy on me, a sinner."

Some ask whether we must use the actual words, since the words are themselves the result of development through practice over five centuries. The answer is yes and no. I suggest that the beginner try reciting the Prayer under the direction of a father or mother as it has been handed down. After a while, if the spiritual father or mother thinks it is okay, then the person might try praying one part or the other.

The fathers of the Philokalia sum it all up. St. Calistas and Ignatius say in their *Directions to Hesychasts*,

> Sitting down in your cell, collect your mind, lead into the path of your breath along which the air enters in, constrain it to enter the heart together with the air, and keep it there. Keep it there, and do not leave it silent or idle; instead give it the following prayer: "Lord, Jesus Christ, Son of God, have mercy on me." Let this be it's constant occupation. . . .
>
> One utters the name of "Lord Jesus"; another of "Jesus Christ"; the third "Christ, Son of God." . . . As regards the words: "have mercy on me" . . . it was added by the holy fathers chiefly for those who are still infants in the work of virtue, the beginners in the imperfect. For the advanced and perfect in Christ are content with any one of these forms.
>
> Beginners may at times say all the words of prayer and at times only part of them, but must pray constantly and within the heart. . . . Refrain from changing the words of prayer too often lest this frequent dropping and changing (of attention from one thing to another) should accustom the mind not to concentrate on one

thing but to deviate from it and so to remain forever not firmly planted in itself; and thus it will bear no fruit.

Gregory of Sinai in his *Instructions to Hesychasts* also confirms that

some of the fathers taught that the prayer should be said in full, . . . others advised saying half, or to alternate, sometimes saying it in full, . . . and sometimes in a shorter form. Yet it is not advisable to pander to laziness by changing the words of the prayer too often, but persist in a certain time as a test of patience. Again some teach saying the prayer with lips, others with and in the mind. In my opinion both are advisable.

WITHOUT CEASING

The goal of the Jesus Prayer is to eventually move beyond practicing at particular times and praying constantly, without ceasing. Sometimes we move our lips, and sometimes we do not, when, for instance, speaking to others. But we pray it without ceasing. Then every moment of every day, day and night, waking and dreaming, we have our entire life transformed by Christ.

The Philokalia and the classic *The Way of the Pilgrim* speak of praying the Prayer from three to five thousand times a day through the use of the prayer rope. Most of us will find this almost impossible outside a monastic or church environment.

So, begin with twenty minutes. It will change your life!

Experience teaches that when the Jesus Prayer is faithfully practiced daily, we begin to see change in the first few days, then another in a week and another in a month. We will also see a change after a few years. After ten or so years of praying faithfully, we will see something happen in our lives that is indelible. Like a sacrament, the Jesus Prayer leaves a permanent mark on the soul. I promise that if prayed well, you will experience a marked change for the better in Christ.

This book represents a few reflections on an ancient tradition. I have written them for a Western audience that is fairly new to the practice of the Jesus Prayer. I have written more fully on this entire tradition in my book *Meditations from Solitude*, an anthology of the teaching of the Philokalia from a Western monastic perspective. I strongly recommend that those interested in further reading seek out a four-volume edition of the Philokalia. If you cannot find one, try the one-volume edition.

APPENDIX

The Roots of the Jesus Prayer

*W*e live in a time when many Christians hunger for something more, something deeper in Christ. Many of us have been well trained in Scripture and apostolic tradition, patristics and patrology, liturgy and sacraments, ecclesiology and ministry. But we have not always been trained very well in the more mystical aspect of meditation and contemplative prayer, which is part of our ancient tradition. Sometimes such things frighten us because we think them overly subjective or downright New Age!

Some actually leave traditional Christianity and investigate Eastern religions that specialize in meditation. Others search the Gnostic Gospels as possible alternatives to a Christianity that has often limited our faith experience to mere head knowledge or emotionalism. But such wanderings are not necessary once we understand that Christians already possess a rich and wonderful heritage of contemplative mystical prayer that dates back to the beginning.

THE CHRISTIAN EAST AND WEST

The Jesus Prayer is one such tradition. It is traced back to St. Hesychios the Priest and St. Diodochos of Photiki (fifth century). They give us the first clear teachings on uniting the name of Jesus with each breath throughout the day. St. Hesychios said,

> We have learned from experience that the one wishes to purify his heart it is truly a great blessing to invoke the name of Jesus. . . . A certain God-given equilibrium is produced . . . through the constant remembrance and invocation of our Lord Jesus Christ. . . . The name of Jesus should be repeated over and over in the heart.

Diodochos said, "Meditate unceasingly upon this glorious and holy name."

From there the Jesus Prayer developed through the Sinai, Mt. Athos and Slavonic Christianity into its present form: "Lord, Jesus Christ, Son of God, have mercy on me, a sinner." Today it is practiced most traditionally by the monks of the Christian East, but especially on Mt. Athos, a most unique monastic republic on a peninsula on Greece's northeastern coast.

The Jesus Prayer comes from the Christian East but has been rediscovered by the Christian West in recent decades. At first this use by the Christian West was resisted by the Orthodox, but they have now accepted it for the most part. The main hesitation had to do with the lack of properly understanding the role of the spiritual father in directing the practitioner of Hesychasm, which used the Jesus Prayer as a primary tool. The old divisions between Orthodoxy and Catholicism also played a part, but those barriers are slowly coming down through mutual dialogue and understanding. Once the fruit was seen as substantially good, even without the normal role of the spiritual father, their resistance was reduced, but the caution still holds true. The place of a good spiritual father or mother (not entirely unlike but not identical to spiritual direction in the West) is most important. But we are wise to remember the admonition "Better to have a spiritual director than no spiritual director, but better not to have a spiritual director than to have a bad one." As we say in the music business, only a fool has himself for a producer! Regardless, the use of the Jesus Prayer has spread in the West, especially in recent decades.

Most Roman Catholics and Protestants are Western Christians. Most Catholics in America are Latin Rite; that is, they use vernacular translations from the Latin translation of Greek and Aramaic liturgical texts. Protestantism is a reform of the real and perceived abuses that existed in the Latin Rite that predominated in Europe in the sixteenth century. Only those who are Orthodox, Eastern or Oriental Christians are truly Eastern. There are historical reasons for this.

St. Paul brought the message of the gospel to the West from the Middle East. Other apostles like St. Thomas took the gospel as far east as the present-day Chennai, India. Paul intentionally targeted Rome, the capital of the greatest Western civilization on earth at that time. Since much of the New Testament is substantially composed of Paul's letters to the churches of Rome, Greece and Asia Minor, our record of Christianity is understandably Western.

As the early church spread throughout the Mediterranean world, first four, then five patriarchates, with bishops directly succeeding apostles, were established in Jerusalem, Alexandria, Antioch and Rome. When the capital of the Roman Empire transferred to Constantinople (the "New Rome"), it became the fifth patriarchate. Ancient Rome held a primary place of honor and leadership due to being the see and place of martyrdom of Peter, and of the martyrdom of Paul. Since there was as yet no New Testament canon of Scripture, when questions of proper teaching of the gospel occurred that divided the churches, Rome was usually asked to resolve the differences.

Ecumenical councils either had the bishop of Rome or his legate in primary attendance. But Rome was the only such patriarchate in the West, so the church in Europe was substantially established and strengthened by a Western patriarchate and tradition. This affected theology as well as ecclesiology.

This decidedly Western orientation has worked pretty well

for us in the West, but it has also limited us. Pope John Paul II spoke of the need to rediscover the way of the East to balance our Western orientation in his encyclical *Ut Unum Sint* or "That They May Be One."

An expression I have frequently employed may be helpful: The church must breathe with both lungs! In the first millennium of the history of Christianity, this expression refers primarily to the relationship between Byzantium and Rome. But today it includes the Eastern and Western churches that span the world. Clearly the vision of the full communion to be sought is that of unity in legitimate diversity. There are, after all, two lungs, but they work in tandem toward the same end—the health of the body.

The Catechism of the Catholic Church says:

This simple invocation of faith developed in the tradition of prayer under many forms in East and West. The most usual formulation, transmitted by the spiritual writers of the Sinai, Syria, and Mt. Athos, is the invocation, "Lord Jesus Christ, Son of God, have mercy on us sinners." It combines the Christological hymn of Philippians 2:6-11 with the cry of the publican and the blind men begging for light. By it the heart is opened to human wretchedness and the Savior's mercy.

The invocation of the holy name of Jesus is the simplest way of praying always. When the holy name is repeated often by a humbly attentive heart, the prayer is not lost by heaping up empty phrases, but holds fast to the word and "brings forth fruit with patience." This prayer is possible "at all times" because it is not one occupation among others but the only occupation: that of loving God, which animates and transfigures every action in Christ Jesus.

Paul says that the church is the "body of Christ" (1 Cor 12:27). Therefore we have two lungs, an Eastern and Western lung. The problem is that most of us in Europe and the Americas have only been breathing from one lung! Unfortunately, we often think that since we are perhaps the wealthiest and even the most numerous, we are also the only expression of the Christian faith. But this is tragically incorrect. In fact, historically, the West grew out of the East, so to deny the East a rightful place in our own spirituality is to seriously impoverish our own spiritual life and Christianity.

HESYCHIA: A WAY OF SACRED STILLNESS

The Jesus Prayer arose out of a tradition in the East called Hesychasm, which practiced the way of hesychia or sacred stillness. St. John Climacus (d. c. 649) writes in his *Ladder of Divine Ascent*, "May the remembrance of Jesus be united with your breathing, and then you will know the value of hesychia." In chapter five we saw Hesychasm had its detractors in the church and that St. Gregory Palamas was the fourteenth-century champion of Hesychasm. In the West

St. Thomas Aquinas likewise defended Hesychasm. Today this different emphasis between East and West is not so pronounced, and the West accepts what the Hesychasts were saying.

There is a profound difference between hesychia in the East and the heresy of Quietism in the West. Hesychasm was an orthodox teaching that gave birth to a radically changed life that became more like Jesus. It confirmed the teaching of the church regarding faith, morality and the celebration of the sacraments. Quietism, on the other hand, stems from the Stoic philosophers and reached its full expression in seventeenth-century France as an attempt to regain the contemplative tradition of Christianity in the West. Under Abbot Fénelon it remained orthodox. But with Madame Guyon it began to drift and reached its full heretical expression with Miguel de Molinos (c. 1628–1697), its primary proponent. He said that we could commit sin while in contemplative quiet, and it would be righteousness for us. Quietists also drifted from the traditional beliefs and disciplines of apostolic Christianity, and radically disengaged from our rightful responsibility for the world.

For our purposes it is enough to say that hesychia is the desired environment and goal of the Jesus Prayer. It is in the sacred stillness that we often find the greatest of God's works in Christ. Stillness, solitude and silence are the best environment for listening to the Word of God and for perceiving his greatest activity in the heart.

A pond is a good analogy for hesychia. When the waters are still, we can look clearly into the depths of the pond, and the surface beautifully reflects an image almost flawlessly. When the waters are agitated both are jeopardized. Sacred stillness allows us to see clearly into the pond of our soul, and allows the pond to reflect the beautiful image of God in Christ.

PRAYER OF THE HEART

The fathers taught that the point of the Jesus Prayer is to find prayer of the heart. The "heart" does not mean the physical organ or even unregenerate emotions and thoughts, but the very center of the human being. It is the deepest spirit and soul. As we have seen, St. Paul speaks of the human being as made up of "spirit, soul, and body" (1 Thess 5:23). The heart builds on the senses, emotions and thoughts of the body and lower soul, but surpasses and then enlivens them all through the awakening of the higher soul and intuitions of the spirit. It moves from the human energies to our deepest essence through a journey through the Uncreated Energies to the Essence of God. Such a journey and experience is describable in part, but for the most part remains beyond human mental understanding alone and therefore beyond description and words. In the West we call it the place of passive contemplation.

The Eastern fathers of the Philokalia use various words and terms that are not easily understood by Westerners today. They use words like *praxis*, *theoria* and *apatheia* to describe work, understanding and contemplative rest. They speak of *dianoia* or *nous* to speak of the difference between discursive thoughts and spiritual mind and reason. These are all ways of trying to describe the basic human need to pass through bodily senses, emotions and thoughts to a deeper spiritual mind in the soul, and even on to intuition in the spirit.

We have a need to pass on from action to prayer and back from prayer into action. We need to go from the bodily and intellectual activities in knowing about God to the contemplative experience of simply being and then knowing God. While this is simple, it is not simplistic. The words and terms are confusing enough, and we sometimes get tripped up trying to sort it all out intellectually. The Jesus Prayer is one traditional way to let go and let God, and simply pass over into the experience through contemplative intuition.

Hesychios says beautifully,

Much like water makes up the sea . . . the Prayer of Jesus, undistracted by thoughts, are the necessary basis for . . . unfathomable inner stillness of the soul, the depths of secret and singular contemplation. . . . These gifts are the guarding of the intellect and the invocation of Jesus Christ, stillness of mind and unbroken by thoughts which even appear to be good, and the capacity to be empty of all thought.

But Diodochos adds, "The intellect requires . . . some task

which will satisfy the need for activity, . . . give it nothing but the prayer, 'Lord Jesus.'"

In other words, in light of modern science we need to slow the distractions of the mind, but we can never stop them completely, so we simplify the mind so it can really focus. Learning to identify and being free of the Eight Thoughts identified by Evagrius Ponticus is one of the accomplishments of the Jesus Prayer.

THE MONASTIC CALL FOR ALL

We learned earlier the word for monk comes from the Greek *monos*, which means "one" or "alone." In the church *monk* is often related to another Greek word, *erēmos*, which means "desert," "wilderness" and "solitude." Jesus went alone into the desert to balance his ministry.

Evagrius wrote rapturously of the monastic calling when he said in his *On Prayer, One Hundred Fifty Three Texts*,

> The monk becomes equal to the angels through prayer, because of his longing to "behold the face of the Father who is in heaven" (cf. Matt. 18:10). . . . Blessed is the monk who regards every man as God after God. . . . Blessed is the monk who looks with great joy on everyone's salvation and progress as if they were his own. . . . A monk is one who is separated from all and united with all. . . . A monk is one who regards himself as linked with every man, through always seeing himself in each.

Monasticism is sometimes portrayed in romantic images

as a uniform and orderly angelic response to a corrupt and worldly church. This is somewhat misleading. It was, rather, an organic impetus of the Spirit that had many manifestations. These ranged from the hermits of the wilderness and desert, to large and small cenobiums in the rural agricultural countryside, to the urban monastic villas and townhouses in cities. It included husbands and wives, families and children, and unmarried singles that usually, but not always, embraced celibacy or continence. The height of the integrated monastic expression was the Celtic model, which included all states of life in a way appropriate to their calling.

While most of my readers are not monastics, many of us are monastics at heart. Like Francis of Assisi we say, "The world is my cloister, my body is my cell, and my soul is the hermit within." He also said that it is not so much that he sought to pray but to become a prayer. Francis said we should preach always, and if we must, use words. These are most attractive ways for all people to live a monastic life no matter the state they find themselves in.

There are three traditional ways to live the monastic life: (1) in strict solitude, (2) in partial solitude in colonies, and (3) in more intense monastic community. The first is the hermit, the second is the social hermit, and the third is a more intense cenobitical monastic community. St. Antony of the Desert (c. 251–356), the father of monks, symbolizes the first. The second, the colony of hermits, symbolized by St. Macarius. The third is the cenobium, symbolized by St.

Pachomius (c. 292–348), the father of the Koinonia. The English words *cenobite* and *cenobitic* are derived from church Latin: *coenobita*, "a cloister brother," which comes from *coenobium*, "a convent," which in turn came from the Greek word *koinobion* (*koinos*, "common" and *bios*, "life"), which means "life in community, monastery."

St. Basil and St. Augustine established a more urban monasticism. Both wrote rules known for their wisdom and moderation, and which are still widely used today in the East and the West.

St. Benedict (c. 480–547) continued a rural cenobitical monasticism that was an alternative society within and alongside secular society. He recognized two good expressions of monastic life. He says in chapter 1 of the Rule of Benedict:

> It is well known that there are four kinds of monks.
> The first kind are the Cenobites:
> those who live in monasteries
> and serve under a rule and an Abbot.
> The second kind are the Anchorites or Hermits:
> those who,
> no longer in the first fervor of their reformation,
> but after long probation in a monastery,
> having learned by the help of many brethren
> how to fight against the devil,
> go out well armed from the ranks of the community
> to the solitary combat of the desert.

They are able now,
with no help save from God,
to fight single-handed against the vices of the flesh
and their own evil thoughts.

St. Romuald of Ravenna (950–c. 1025/27), founder of the Camaldolese, and St. Bruno of Cologne (c. 1030–1101), founder of the Carthusians, brought the Eastern semi- or social eremitism back into the West. They allow for cenobites and hermits who live in a scattering of cells around a common chapel, refectory (monastic dining room) and monastic buildings, as well as recluses who live in complete solitude, except for those who come to them for spiritual direction.

On Mt. Athos (monasteries founded in the ninth century), where the Jesus Prayer is emphasized, all three are seen. There are cenobiums, where monks train together. After learning these basics they can move into greater, but partial, solitude in the sketes (Greek, *skētē*) and kellions (where we get our word *cell*, or the place where heaven comes to earth) that for the most part exist under a cenobium, but with their own spiritual father.

These three monastic ways have much to teach us. We all need the solitude of the hermit to balance the crowded modern city, the support of community when we feel most alone, and the balance between solitude and community to bring genuine health and happiness to us all.

THE PHILOKALIA

The greatest source for discovering the traditional teaching of the Jesus Prayer is found in the Philokalia or "the study of the beautiful." There have been several collections under this title, the earliest tracing itself to Origen, though we do not have an extant copy of it. The one we refer to is traceable to the eighteenth-century collection by St. Nikodemos of the Holy Mountain and St. Makarius of Corinth. These works were individually known in the monastic culture of Greek Orthodox Christianity before the Philokalia. The earliest translations included a Slavonic translation of selected texts by Paisius Velichkovsky in 1793, a Russian translation by Ignatius Bryanchaninov in 1857 and a five-volume translation into Russian by St. Theophan the Recluse in 1877. There were subsequent Romanian, Italian and French translations.

After the Bible collections of Scripture, this collection of the monastic fathers on "prayer of the heart" is considered most important. *The Way of the Pilgrim* says:

> "Is it then more important than the Holy Bible?" I asked.
>
> "No, it is neither more important nor holier than the Bible, but it contains clear exposition of the ideas that are mysteriously presented in the Bible and are not easy for our finite mind to understand."

Bibliography

Aquilina, Mike. *The Mass of the Early Christians*. Huntington, IN: Our Sunday Visitor, 2001.

The Faith of the Early Fathers. 3 vols. Translated by William Jurgens. Collegeville, MN: Liturgical Press, 1998.

Lossky, Vladimir. *The Mystical Theology of the Eastern Church*. Yonkers, NY: Saint Vladimir's Seminary Press, 1997.

Maloney, George S. *A Theology of Uncreated Energies of God*. Marquette, MI: Marquette University Press, 1978.

Nikodimos of the Holy Mountain and Markarios of Corinth, comps. *The Philokalia: The Complete Text*. Translated by G. E. H. Palmer, Philip Sherrard and Kallistos Ware. London: Faber & Faber, 1995.

Papandrea, James L. *Reading the Early Church Fathers: From the Didache to Nicaea*. Mahwah, NJ: Paulist Press, 2012.

The Rule of St. Benedict. Edited by Timothy Fry. Collegeville, MN: Liturgical Press, 1981.

Talbot, John Michael. *Come to the Quiet: The Principles of Christian Meditation*. New York: Tarcher/Putnam, 2002.

The Way of a Pilgrim and The Pilgrim Continues His Way. Translated by Helen Bocovcin. New York: Image/Doubleday, 1978.

Suggested Reading

Mary

Benedict XVI. *Mary: The Church at the Source.* Translated by Adrian Walker. San Francisco: Ignatius Press, 2005.

Gambero, Luigi. *Mary and the Fathers of the Church: The Blessed Virgin Mary in Patristic Thought.* San Francisco: Ignatius Press, 1999.

Gambero, Luigi. *Mary in the Middle Ages: The Blessed Virgin Mary in the Thought of Medieval Latin Theologians.* San Francisco: Ignatius Press, 2005.

Deification

Keating, Daniel A. *Deification and Grace.* Ave Maria, FL: Sapientia Press of Ave Maria University, 2007.

Russell, Norman. *The Doctrine of Deification in the Greek Patristic Tradition.* Oxford Early Christian Studies. New York: Oxford University Press, 2004.

Liturgy

Gregorios, Hieromonk. *The Divine Liturgy: A Commentary in the Light of the Fathers.* Translated by Elizabeth Theokritoff. Columbia, MO: Newrome Press, 2012.

Jungmann, Joseph A., S.J. *The Mass of the Roman Rite: Its Origins and Development*. 2 vols. Notre Dame, IN: Ave Maria Press, 2012.

Taft, Robert F. *The Byzantine Rite: A Short History*. American Essays in Liturgy. Collegeville, MN: The Order of St. Benedict, 1992.

Christology

McGuckin, J. A. *St. Cyril of Alexandria: The Christological Controversy Its History, Theology, and Texts*. Yonkers, NY: St Vladimir's Seminary Press, 2004.

Schonborn, Christoph Cardinal. *God Sent His Son*. San Francisco: Ignatius Press, 2010.

formatio

TRADITION. EXPERIENCE. TRANSFORMATION.

Formatio books from InterVarsity Press follow the rich tradition of the church in the journey of spiritual formation. These books are not merely about being informed, but about being transformed by Christ and conformed to his image. Formatio stands in InterVarsity Press's evangelical publishing tradition by integrating God's Word with spiritual practice and by prompting readers to move from inward change to outward witness. InterVarsity Press uses the chambered nautilus for Formatio, a symbol of spiritual formation because of its continual spiral journey outward as it moves from its center. We believe that each of us is made with a deep desire to be in God's presence. Formatio books help us to fulfill our deepest desires and to become our true selves in light of God's grace.